BERNARD SHAW
A Guide to Research

Other books by Stanley Weintraub about Bernard Shaw

An Unfinished Novel by Bernard Shaw, ed.

Private Shaw and Public Shaw: A Dual Portrait of Lawrence of Arabia and G.B.S.

The Court Theatre, ed.

"Cashel Byron's Profession" by Bernard Shaw, ed.

Shaw: An Autobiography 1856–1898, ed.

Shaw: An Autobiography 1898–1950. The Playwright Years, ed.

"Saint Joan" by Bernard Shaw, ed.

Journey to Heartbreak: Bernard Shaw 1914–1918

Bernard Shaw's Nondramatic Literary Criticism, ed.

"Saint Joan": Fifty Years After—1923/24—1973/74, ed.

The Portable Bernard Shaw, ed.

Heartbreak House: A Facsimile of the Original Typescript, ed. with Anne Wright

The Playwright and the Pirate: Bernard Shaw and Frank Harris, a Correspondence by Bernard Shaw and Frank Harris, ed.

The Unexpected Shaw: Biographical Approaches to G.B.S. and His Work

Bernard Shaw: The Diaries. 1885–1897, ed., 2 vols.

Bernard Shaw on the London Art Scene, 1885–1950, ed.

BERNARD SHAW

A Guide to Research

Stanley Weintraub

The Pennsylvania State University Press
University Park, Pennsylvania

Library of Congress Cataloging-in-Publication Data

Weintraub, Stanley, 1929–
Bernard Shaw : a guide to research / Stanley Weintraub.
p. cm.
Includes indexes.
ISBN 0-271-00831-8 (alk. paper)
1. Shaw, Bernard, 1856–1950—Bibliography. I. Title.
Z8814.5.W44 1992
[PR5366]
016.822′912—dc20 91–41779
CIP

Printed in the United States of America

It is the policy of The Pennsylvania State University Press to use acid-free paper for the first printing of all clothbound books. Publications on uncoated stock satisfy the minimum requirements of American National Standard for Information Sciences—Permanence of Paper for Printed Library Materials, ANSI Z39.48–1984.

Contents

Preface 1

1 Provenance and Copyright 4
2 Bibliographies 7
3 Editions 9
4 Biographies and Autobiographies 19
5 Early Criticism 33
6 General Critical Evaluations 37
7 The Novels and Other Fiction 51
8 Early Musical, Dramatic, and Literary Journalism 56
9 Criticism of Individual Plays 60
10 Criticism in Languages Other Than English 121
11 Shaw in Fiction 124
12 Influence and Reputation 128
13 A Guide to Acronyms and Abbreviations 142

Index of Authors 144
Index of Works 150
Subject Index 153

require several very large volumes, and a mere unculled listing is not a guide to useful research.

Necessarily this is a subjective overview by one scholar, albeit one in his fifth decade of coping with Shaw studies. Its emphasis is on post-Shavian decades of research and criticism, which have rendered earlier work less authoritative. Recent research has undermined many earlier hypotheses. Some facts have turned out not to be facts; earlier transcripts of manuscripts and letters have been rendered obsolete by their originals; new material continues to surface to alter our readings of works or our perspectives upon Shaw's life and ideas. Publications of solely historical interest are, nevertheless, cited, although not every book or article, and weight is given to work in English.

Few book or play reviews are covered here unless they contribute to critical understanding in a significant way. With two exceptions, dissertations do not appear unless they have been made accessible by book or article publication and meet the standard of significance. (What is accepted as degree-worthy research is sometimes, in its triviality and redundancy, questionable.) Inevitably there are redundancies in scholarship, and in some cases it is useful and even necessary to go over much-plowed terrain, but unless something substantial is produced by the effort it goes unnoticed here. Yet vast areas of potentially valuable research remain, as in old maps of the world, *terra incognita*. Some of these are noted for future investigators.

In the interest of efficiency, names and titles are usually abbreviated after an initial entry. A listing of journal abbreviations using accepted codes appears in an appendix. Publishers do not normally appear, as any search of the literature by name, title, and date will furnish such data.

I welcome suggestions from scholars about books and articles to include in a future update—either new publications or overlooked ones with significance to our understanding of Shaw and his work. Obviously I have excluded most general considerations of his times, his places of activity, and his friends, yet often these

Contents

Preface 1

1 Provenance and Copyright 4
2 Bibliographies 7
3 Editions 9
4 Biographies and Autobiographies 19
5 Early Criticism 33
6 General Critical Evaluations 37
7 The Novels and Other Fiction 51
8 Early Musical, Dramatic, and Literary Journalism 56
9 Criticism of Individual Plays 60
10 Criticism in Languages Other Than English 121
11 Shaw in Fiction 124
12 Influence and Reputation 128
13 A Guide to Acronyms and Abbreviations 142

Index of Authors 144
Index of Works 150
Subject Index 153

For my brother, Herb, who in 1951
sent three Shaw paperbacks to me
while I was in Army service in
Korea, thereby introducing me
to G.B.S.

Preface

However controversial in his own lifetime and since his death at ninety-four in 1950, Bernard Shaw is an artist of classical standing. His books are read and reprinted; his plays are performed, even resorted to by producers when all else at the box office fails; his personality is of compelling interest; his every work is scrutinized by scholars and examined in increasing numbers of articles and books.

An attempt at orderly reconsideration of research on Shaw was made in 1975 in a monograph-long chapter I prepared for *Anglo-Irish Writers: A Guide to Research*, published by the Modern Language Association. A supplement was called for, and was released in 1983 as *Recent Research on Anglo-Irish Writers*. A full revision was authorized in the later 1980s for publication about 1990, but the effort miscarried as scholarly projects by committees sometimes do. However, the Shaw section, burgeoning as it had through continuous updating, took on a life of its own, and reemerges here with entries into 1992, and indications of work in progress beyond that. To cover everything, however, would require several very large volumes, and a mere unculled listing is not a guide to useful research.

Necessarily this is a subjective overview by one scholar, albeit one in his fifth decade of coping with Shaw studies. Its emphasis is on post-Shavian decades of research and criticism, which have rendered earlier work less authoritative. Recent research has undermined many earlier hypotheses. Some facts have turned out not to be facts; earlier transcripts of manuscripts and letters have been rendered obsolete by their originals; new material continues to surface to alter our readings of works or our perspectives upon Shaw's life and ideas. Publications of solely historical interest are, nevertheless, cited, although not every book or article, and weight is given to work in English.

Few book or play reviews are covered here unless they contribute to critical understanding in a significant way. With two exceptions, dissertations do not appear unless they have been made accessible by book or article publication and meet the standard of significance. (What is accepted as degree-worthy research is sometimes, in its triviality and redundancy, questionable.) Inevitably there are redundancies in scholarship, and in some cases it is useful and even necessary to go over much-plowed terrain, but unless something substantial is produced by the effort it goes unnoticed here. Yet vast areas of potentially valuable research remain, as in old maps of the world, *terra incognita*. Some of these are noted for future investigators.

In the interest of efficiency, names and titles are usually abbreviated after an initial entry. A listing of journal abbreviations using accepted codes appears in an appendix. Publishers do not normally appear, as any search of the literature by name, title, and date will furnish such data.

I welcome suggestions from scholars about books and articles to include in a future update—either new publications or overlooked ones with significance to our understanding of Shaw and his work. Obviously I have excluded most general considerations of his times, his places of activity, and his friends, yet often these studies contribute profoundly to our perspectives of the context in which he lived and wrote.

This is not a missionary work—to lure scholars and readers into the world of Shavian research. It is a preachment, in depth, to the curious and the converted. Yet I hope that other hands will take up the challenges as the generations of scholars represented here put down their pens and switch off their computers. Bernard Shaw remains a feast as well as a test; he offers us a subtext as well as a text; and as his works now begin to enter the public domain he is likely to be read and performed more often than in his heyday. This guide to research is prepared in that expectation.

Many scholars have contributed to this guide, but any errors are mine, not theirs. Among my collaborators, to whom I offer my gratitude here, are Charles A. Berst, Charles A. Carpenter, Jr., Fred D. Crawford, Bernard F. Dukore, Leon H. Hugo, Dan H. Laurence, Frederick P. W. McDowell, and John R. Pfeiffer.

1

Provenance and Copyright

Visiting Bernard Shaw's country home at Ayot St. Lawrence for the National Trust, to which it had been willed, shortly after Shaw's death in November 1950, Sir Harold Nicolson was both excited and appalled. The place was too remote and unpretentious for someone of Shaw's inflated reputation. "The furniture," he wrote to his wife, Vita Sackville-West, "was lodging-house. Not a single good piece. But darling, it was thrilling. Shaw was there. In the garden hut he was there still, . . . in the shape of ashes in the rose-bed and garden-paths, white ashes. . . ." But apart from the physical evidence of the man, Nicolson found the prospects for the National Trust rather bleak. Shaw's work was hardly up to the furniture, or to the "dull and undistinguished" Hertfordshire house. "I am not happy about it," he noted in his diary. "I do not think that Shaw will be a great literary figure in 2000 A.D. He is an amazingly brilliant contemporary, but not in the [Thomas] Hardy class." Yet Shaw had coolly envisioned that prospect, offering his house to the nation as a "trifle," to be sold off in twenty years if the Trust "found that his name was forgotten."

The property was accepted with some qualms, and most of the books and manuscripts not necessary for display, along with the papers he had left at his London flat in Whitehall Court, were moved to the British Museum (now Library). Although his own collections represented the largest archive of his life and work, it had been for years far from the only one. Because Shaw was a public figure for so long—perhaps the most famous and the most influential writer of his time—recipients of many thousands of his letters preserved them, and his manuscript writings were also marketable early in his career. Shaw also saved drafts and scraps himself, and much corespondence *to* him. His own papers—including the bulk of his correspondence and the largest collection of his play manuscripts—are now largely at the British Library, one of the three residuary legatees of his will. Many of his play drafts and the largest collection of his own letters are at the University of Texas. His diaries, appointment books, and some business records as well as his letters to Beatrice and Sidney Webb are at the British Library of Political and Economic Science (London School of Economics); however, two of his three income ledgers, covering the most productive years of his career (through 1928), are at Texas. The manuscripts of four of his novels and the fragment of an uncompleted novel are at the National Library of Ireland. Substantial collections of Shaw manuscripts, letters, and printed materials exist also at the New York Public Library (Berg Collection), the University of North Carolina at Chapel Hill, the Houghton Library at Harvard University, the Burgunder Collection at the Cornell University Library (especially rich in rehearsal copies, leaflets, and pamphlets), the Butler Collection at the Bucknell University Library, the Strong Collection at California State University at Fullerton, Yale University, the Mugar Memorial Library at Boston University, the Albert Collection at Brown University, and the library of Nuffield College, Oxford University, which houses the Fabian Society archive.

An index to eighty-five major Shaw manuscripts and their archival locations appears as part *J* in vol. 2 of Dan H. Laurence's *Bernard Shaw: A Bibliography* (1973). Hundreds of other public and private collections contain unlisted manuscript holdings of letters and other documents.

Fewer and fewer valuable Shaw materials remain in private hands, and these are gradually proceeding into public collections through donation, dispersal of estates, and sale. A rich and continuing source of manuscript data exists in the runs of auction and sale catalogs of past and present major firms from about 1930 to the present—Maggs, Sotheby, Christie, Anderson, Richards, and others. Often, large blocks of quotation have appeared, taken from letters and other manuscripts offered which have then fallen into private hands and become inaccessible. Often, too, entire letters have been reproduced in facsimile. Although in a few cases the holograph is misread or a typographical error garbles a text, this hoard of documentation is all the more valuable because it is largely unindexed and difficult to get at and use. Some libraries retain sets of such publications.

A spurt of Shaw publications may ensue as the copyright owners exercise their rights before copyrights in force at Shaw's death expire in the year 2000. Once such publications go into the public domain, a deluge of reprints is inevitable. Here it should be noted that works in manuscript at Shaw's death and copyrighted in later years, such as play manuscripts and unpublished essays and letters, begin their published lives with new copyrights. Under the old copyright law an unpublished work had a "common law" protection that lasted indefinitely. Under the new American copyright law, which follows international copyright, the period is defined: Shaw's unpublished manuscripts are protected until at least 31 December 2002. If they are published before that date, they will be protected by copyright until 31 December 2027. Thereafter, the manuscripts will be in the public domain.

2

Bibliographies

The two-volume bibliography by Dan H. Laurence remains the starting point for almost any Shaw research, although like any bibliography of its scope there are lacunae to be filled in by later revisions. Its coverage excluded most translations and many first appearances of Shaw material (largely letters) in books by others and in auction and sale catalogs, but the net is cast widely: books and ephemeral publications, rough proofs and rehearsal copies, contributions to books (but incomplete as noted above), works edited by Shaw, contributions to newspapers and periodicals (3,975 of these, yet some escape), stereotyped postcards, blurbs, broadcasts, recordings, and manuscripts with their locations. A final section lists separate works *on* Shaw through 1982. Although earlier and fragmentary bibliographies exist, *Bernard Shaw: A Bibliography* supersedes all others.

A three-volume *G. B. Shaw: An Annotated Bibliography of Writings About Him*, furnishes abstracts and citations through 1980. The first segment, compiled and edited by J. P. Wearing (1986), includes 3,676 entries from 1871 through 1930. The second, by

Elsie B. Adams with Donald C. Haberman (1987), encompasses 2,394 entries from 1931 through 1956. The third, by D. C. Haberman (1986), contains 2,677 entries from 1957 through 1980. "A Continuing Checklist of Shaviana"—which lists new editions of Shaw as well as secondary bibliographical items from books, periodicals, theses, dissertations, films, and recordings—appeared three times a year in the *Shaw Review*, which began its checklists in 1950. In 1981 this checklist began appearing in *SHAW: The Annual of Bernard Shaw Studies*, which continues the *Shaw Review* in augmented book format. Its compiler is John R. Pfeiffer.

3

Editions

The *Bodley Head Edition of Collected Plays and Their Prefaces* (7 vols., 1970–74) contains not only all the plays and prefaces published by Shaw in his lifetime in their finally revised texts* but (in vol. 7) fragments of the *Passion Play* (1878), *The Cassone* (1889), and *The Garden of the Hesperides* (ca. 1930s), plus the full texts of a dramatization of Ethel Voynich's *The Gadfly* (1898) and a number of short plays and exercises in dialogue, some hitherto unpublished or uncollected, which Shaw frugally elected not to discard. The edition (in the U.S., entitled *Collected Plays with Their Prefaces,* 1975) also contains data regarding composition, publication, and first performances in English as well as miscellaneous Shavian pronouncements on each play in the form of press

*Also crucial to any study of Shaw's dramaturgy are not only the earlier published texts but Shaw's printed rehearsal proof copies of his plays in wrappers for actors, directors, translators, and other theater uses. The practice began with *Blanco Posnet* in 1909 and provides variant texts—sometimes the only record of some dialogue—since Shaw amended his texts frequently from standing type before first publication.

releases, self-drafted interviews, program notes, and letters to editors. Although there are typographical and textual errors in the plays and prefaces, it nevertheless supersedes all previous collections. A new *Complete Prefaces* (in 3 vols., ed. Dan H. Laurence and Daniel J. Leary) is in the process of publication (1992–).

A valuable adjunct to the Shavian dramatic texts is the ten-volume *Concordance to the Plays and Prefaces of Bernard Shaw,* by E. Dean Bevan (1971), which is in effect a dictionary of Shavian quotations as well as a concordance that uses a computerized "keyword" system which places each word centrally in a substantial context. The text used is the superseded Collected Edition, which means (since another concordance is unlikely soon) that cross-references to it from the Bodley Head text will continue to be needed.

Collected Screenplays (1980), edited by Bernard F. Dukore, includes scripts for *Saint Joan, Pygmalion, Arms and the Man, Major Barbara, Caesar and Cleopatra* (with some discarded scenes), a fragment of a *Devil's Disciple* scenario, and prefaces for cinema audiences to *Pygmalion* and *Major Barbara.* Dukore's lengthy introduction is itself a substantial piece of criticism. (Other Shaw plays filmed and televised have had scripts by others, and the filmed *Joan* did not use Shaw's much superior screenplay.) It is useful here to note the other major studies of Shaw as writer for the cinema, Donald P. Costello's *The Serpent's Eye* (1965) and Marjorie Deans's *Meeting at the Sphinx: Gabriel Pascal's Production of Bernard Shaw's "Caesar and Cleopatra"* (1946), which includes an unshot scene. Several Shavian filmscript texts also appear in the Costello book.

Bernard Shaw. Early Texts: Play Manuscripts in Facsimile, under the general editorship of Dan H. Laurence (12 vols., 1980–81), very likely to be known as the Garland edition, includes all the early play manuscripts in the Shaw archive in the British Library that were originally drafted in longhand, plus the drastically revised typescript of *Heartbreak House,* of which the shorthand draft is lost. Analytical introductions by individual scholars accompany each play. *Widowers' Houses* (which includes the Berg Collection's complete holograph MS) is edited by Jerald E. Bringle; *The Philanderer* (including a deleted act) by Julius Novick; *Mrs Warren's Profession,* heavily revised, by Margot Peters; and *Arms and the Man,* as it appeared before Shaw reordered scenes, by Norma Jenckes. *Candida* and its farcical inversion, *How He Lied to Her Husband,* are paired in J. Percy Smith's volume, and *You Never Can Tell* is edited by D. J. Leary. Robert F. Whitman's edition of *The Devil's Disciple* includes an early shorthand sketch on Shaw's ideas for the play in transition, which was first drafted without its American Revolution venue, and J. L. Wisenthal's volume combines two history plays, *The Man of Destiny* and *Caesar and Cleopatra.* Rodelle Weintraub's edition of *Captain Brassbound's Conversion* shows Shaw's early concern with accents and dialects and includes a chantey to be sung; and *Major Barbara,* in B. F. Dukore's edition, includes the original final scene as well as the substantially rewritten one. Margery Morgan's edition of *The Doctor's Dilemma* includes designs for the first production. *Heartbreak House,* coedited by Stanley Weintraub and Anne Wright, is a much longer text than the published play, having a new beginning, a new ending (both including shorthand revisions), and Shaw's own sketches for stage settings. The editors examine the plays from the standpoint of the manuscripts, the sources, and the intentions revealed in the working out of the text and provide other insights that supplement references to individual plays in later pages here. Some of these essays are the best individual studies yet of particular plays.

A smaller-scale project to produce facsimile volumes of the extant novels (only scraps of *Love among the Artists* survive) has, unfortunately, been aborted, but its potential value remains. Shaw's later "improvements" to the early novels have created published anachronisms, especially in the case of *Immaturity* (written 1879). The real Shaw of 1879–82 exists in the surviving manuscripts of the early fiction.

Shaw's dramatic principles, as opposed to his practice, emerge in "Bernard Shaw at Oxford: GBS's Lecture on Playwriting"

(*ShawR,* 1979), which salvages the transcript of Shaw's March 1914 lecture from the *Oxford Times* of 6 March. The longest reconstruction of the talk, which was delivered from a few note cards, it describes Shaw's techniques of causation and of theatricality.

In Shaw's lifetime the limited Collected Edition (33 vols., 1930–37), called the Ayot St. Lawrence Edition (30 vols., 1930–32) in the United States, was followed in England by the Constable Standard Edition. Each published the five novels followed by the plays to date, and nonfictional prose collections and compilations such as the three volumes each of *Our Theatres in the Nineties, Music in London, What I Really Wrote about the War, Doctors' Delusions, Crude Criminology, Sham Education, Essays in Fabian Socialism,* and *Short Stories, Scraps and Shavings.* These were supplemented through Shaw's remaining career by additional Standard Edition titles (*Sixteen Self Sketches,* 1949, was the last), including volumes of new plays.

Not included in the collected works was *Table-Talk of G.B.S.: Conversations on Things in General between George Bernard Shaw and His Biographer* (1925). Originally a ninety-five-page Shaw manuscript, it was never a dialogue except on paper. Among Shavian publications of note that appeared separately from the Collected and Standard editions in his last decades was his last (1948) edition of *Fabian Essays,* which he had first edited and contributed to in 1889, and of which he had overseen additional augmented editions in 1908 and 1920.

Posthumous collections of Shavian writings have continued to enlarge the prose canon: *Shaw and Society: An Anthology and a Symposium* (ed. C.E.M. Joad, 1953), extracts from Shaw's writings on society; *Shaw on Theatre* (ed. E. J. West, 1958), uncollected writings on drama; *How to Become a Musical Critic* (ed. Dan H. Laurence, 1960), uncollected writings on music; *Platform and Pulpit* (ed. Dan H. Laurence, 1961), uncollected speeches; *The Matter with Ireland* (ed. Dan H. Laurence and David H. Greene, 1962), uncollected writings on Ireland; *The Religious Speeches of Bernard Shaw* (ed. Warren S. Smith, 1963), lay sermons and speeches; *The Rationalization of Russia by Bernard Shaw* (ed. Harry M. Geduld, 1964), Shaw on his U.S.S.R. trip; *Selected Nondramatic Writings of Bernard Shaw* (ed. Dan H. Laurence, 1965); *Shaw on Religion* (ed. W. S. Smith, 1967); *The Road to Equality: Ten Unpublished Lectures and Essays, 1884–1918* (ed. Louis Crompton, 1971), lectures, mostly early, on socialism and economics; *Bernard Shaw's Nondramatic Literary Criticism* (ed. S. Weintraub, 1972), including an early—1887—and lengthy Shaw lecture on realism in fiction. All of Shaw's 111 book reviews in the *Pall Mall Gazette* in the 1880s are collected and annotated in *Bernard Shaw's Book Reviews Originally Published in the Pall Mall Gazette from 1885 to 1888,* ed. Brian F. Tyson (1991). A further volume will collect all later literary reviews.

Other Shavian writings, particularly early efforts, have been published in journals. Among the most notable (ed. L. Crompton and Hilayne Cavanaugh) is his 1884 lecture on Shakespeare's *Troilus and Cressida,* which exceeds in length among Shaw's writings on the Bard even Shaw's Preface to *The Dark Lady of the Sonnets* (*ShawR,* 1971). *Bernard Shaw: Practical Politics* (ed. Lloyd Hubenka, 1976) collects post-1906 lectures and articles. *G. Bernard Shaw 1856–1950: Photographer and Critic* (ed. Bill Jay and Margaret Moore, 1987) brings together Shaw's reviews of camera exhibitions and prefaces to catalogues.

A late work, *The Black Girl in Search of God* (1933), appears in a definitive text (ed. Dan H. Laurence) in the Penguin 1977 edition, which is otherwise a corrected reprint of the 1934 collection (with the lesser tales). The revised text is also in the *Portable Bernard Shaw* (minus preface). Not so much a text as a collection of rehearsal notes and sketches is B. F. Dukore's edition, *Bernard Shaw's* Arms and the Man: *A Composite Production Book* (1982), which illuminates the playwright's ideas for productions he personally supervised. Defeating categorization is *Flyleaves* (ed. Dan H. Laurence and D. J. Leary, 1977), which presents the results of Shaw's cranky decision, at ninety-three, to create artificial book rarities by writing long inscriptions in books he was consigning to the auction rooms. The entries are intriguing "last words"—especially on Bunyan, Shakespeare, T. E. Lawrence, Elgar, and Malory, reproduced in full.

Shaw's versifying is ubiquitous, and printings of his usually flippant doggerel, ballads, and satires are too numerous to list. The most extensive posthumous publication is S. Weintraub's "Ballads by Shaw: The Anonymous *Star* Versifier of 1888–89," *SHAW* 9 (1989); one, "From the Housetops," was previously unidentified. In an abandoned appointment book (BL) for 1873, W. S. Smith notes in "An Early GBS Love Poem," *ShawR* (1967), is a Shelleyan love poem about a girl left behind in Ireland ("But my fate brought me shortly to Britain / Away from her gaze . . ."). A penciled rough draft in twelve stanzas, it has little quality as verse but much in the mystery it evokes about how little we really know of Shaw's early years. Other verses have appeared in books and articles, none of them suggesting that Shaw had any promise as a poet, but rather an Irishman's love for limericks and light verse. The subject remains to be more fully explored. In book form the only collection, purportedly by Shaw, is *Lady, wilt thou love me? Eighteen Love Poems for Ellen Terry* (1980), ed. Jack Werner. The handwriting of the poems (eighteen of twenty extant verses are printed) is described as "disguised." The dubious collection is disowned by Shaw's executors and labeled by Laurence a "misattribution" in the Shaw *Bibliography.*

Shaw's private letters have been appearing in newspapers, journals, and books of biography and memoirs since his earliest public years. It is likely that the number he wrote in seventy years of public life is well into six figures, and that tens of thousands are still extant, most now in library collections. The first and only substantial publication of the correspondence is the *Collected Letters of Bernard Shaw* (ed. Dan H. Laurence, 1965–88), which brings together in four volumes fewer than three thousand of the letters (vol. 1, 1874–97; vol. 2, 1898–1910; vol. 3, 1911–25; vol. 4, 1926–50). Earlier collections, several of them incomplete or with slightly flawed texts, have been primarily those addressed to a single correspondent: *Letters from George*

Bernard Shaw to Miss Alma Murray (Mrs. Alfred Forman) (1927); *More Letters . . .* (1932); *Ellen Terry and Bernard Shaw: A Correspondence* (ed. Christopher St. John, 1931); *Florence Farr, Bernard Shaw, W. B. Yeats: Letters* (ed. Clifford Bax, 1941)—a useful supplement is Josephine Johnson, *Florence Farr: Bernard Shaw's "New Woman"* (1975); *Bernard Shaw and Mrs. Patrick Campbell: Their Correspondence* (ed. Alan Dent, 1952); *Advice to a Young Critic* [R. Golding Bright] *and Other Letters* (ed. E. J. West, 1955); *In a Great Tradition: Tribute to Dame Laurentia McLachlan, Abbess of Stanbrook* (ed. the Nuns of Stanbrook, 1956), where a chapter is devoted to her correspondence with Shaw; and D. Felicitas Corrigan's *The Nun, the Infidel, and the Superman* (1985), which published both sides of the exchange. *Bernard Shaw's Letters to Granville Barker* (ed. C. B. Purdom, 1957) is textually unreliable, and many letters are reproduced more accurately in *CL* vols. 2 and 3 and in Eric Salmon's edition of Barker's letters, *Granville Barker and His Correspondents* (1985), which is of great Shavian significance in other respects as well. *To a Young Actress: The Letters of Bernard Shaw to Molly Tompkins* (ed. Peter Tompkins, 1960) lacks an index but does not lack interest and should be examined in the light of C. A. Berst's "Shaw, Molly Tompkins, and Italy, 1921–1950," *SHAW* 5, *Shaw Abroad* (ed. R. Weintraub, 1985). The biographical essay utilizes the original MSS of all the extant letters.

Also supplementing the *Collected Letters* are *Bernard Shaw and Alfred Douglas: A Correspondence* (ed. Mary Hyde, 1982); *The Playwright and the Pirate: Bernard Shaw and Frank Harris* (ed. S. Weintraub, 1982); *Bernard Shaw's Letters to Siegfried Trebitsch,* his German translator over a lifetime (ed. Samuel Weiss, 1986); *Bernard Shaw, Lady Gregory, and the Abbey* (ed. Dan H. Laurence and Nicholas Grene, 1992); and "Ezra Pound and G. B. Shaw: A Long Wordy War," by Breon Mitchell, *JJQ* (1986). A sampling of letters to Shaw and some of his responses is found in *Dear Mr. Shaw* (ed. Vivian Elliot, 1987), which is useful although it is not indexed and some letters are undated or misdated. Also, numerous stage and film biographies and autobiographies (of

Edith Evans, Raymond Massey, and others) continue to include Shaw letters, and additional full exchanges between Shaw and other associates can be expected to appear. Among the planned correspondences are Shaw's exchanges with H. G. Wells, Gilbert Murray, William Archer, Lady Astor, John Farleigh, Gabriel Pascal, and Augustin Hamon. Further, Shaw's letters to the press (only the unpublished ones appear in *CL*) have been sampled in *Agitations: Letters to the Press, 1875–1950* (ed. Dan H. Laurence and James Rambeau, 1985). Laurence is editing Shaw's uncollected letters on theatrical subjects, and additional collections will appear on publishing matters (including letters to translators, printers, and designers) and on socialist politics and theory.

As far as accurate texts of Shaw letters are concerned, all transcripts prior to *Collected Letters* must be accepted with great caution, even—perhaps especially—those edited, vetted, or made by Shaw himself, who rewrote his letters when circumstances were propitious.

The complete and definitive music criticism has been brought together and edited by Dan H. Laurence in *Shaw's Music* (3 vols., 1981). It includes articles from the *World* and the *Star* that Shaw omitted from his own collections; other criticism, earlier and later, including unsigned reviews in the *Hornet* (1876–77), the *Dramatic Review* (1885), and the *Pall Mall Gazette* (1885–88); and miscellaneous essays on musical subjects. Shaw's art journalism from the *Star,* the *World, Truth,* and other publications from the 1880s and 1890s, augmented by his later writings on art subjects, is collected as *Bernard Shaw on the London Art Scene, 1885–1950* (ed. S. Weintraub, 1989); while his collected drama reviews and other theatrical journalism appears as *The Drama Observed* (ed. B. F. Dukore, 1993), with texts corrected from earlier reprintings and first reprintings of previously fugitive material.

Collections of Shaw's writings on subjects that cohere into book form are likely to increase. *Shaw on Dickens* (ed. Dan H. Laurence and Martin Quinn, 1985),* an example of the genre,

*"Shaw and Dickens," ed. M. Quinn (*ShawR,* 1977), begins with a "Shaw/Dickens File" compiled by Edgar Rosenberg on the multifarious Shavian allusions to

includes, with previously published material, the substantial but incomplete British Library manuscript of "From Dickens to Ibsen," an early lecture from which G.B.S. extracted material he later used in writing about Ibsen.

Although the body of Shaw's writings about Ibsen remain uncollected, in *Shaw and Ibsen* (1979) J. L. Wisenthal includes *The Quintessence of Ibsenism* in a definitive text, the third and final edition of 1922, to which are added the numerous alterations from the 1891 and 1913 editions and the appendix to the 1891 edition, deleted in later texts. There are also copious annotations, a historical introduction, and several shorter Shavian pieces on Ibsen written both before and after 1891, including Shaw's original Fabian lecture that was the germ of *Quintessence.* Wisenthal's introduction is penetrating and valuable—the best single essay on Shaw and Ibsen. In Ibsen, Wisenthal claims, "Shaw saw the possibility of a drama of . . . moral indictment" and "the possibility of combining surface realism and symbolic non-realistic methods. . . . In 1891 Shaw saw mostly the realistic surface in Ibsen's plays, and this is reflected in his own work of this period. In 1912–13 (when revising the *Quintessence*) he saw more of the non-naturalistic symbolic and poetic techniques, and this is reflected in *Heartbreak House.*"

F.P.W. McDowell's "Fountainhead and Fountain: Ibsen and Shaw" (*ShawR,* 1980), which uses Wisenthal's study as a springboard, is highly perceptive on Shaw's use of Ibsen and on Shaw's concept of his own plays as tragicomedies—a reason, McDowell suggests, for Shaw's preference for the dark comedies of Shakespeare. Thus to McDowell there are tensions in Shaw's plays that appear Ibsenian, "though Ibsen's vision is, of course, even more sardonic and satiric than Shaw's. With the familiarity that has overtaken Shaw's plays and with the sentimentalizing of many of

Dickens (continued in *SHAW* 2 [1982]) and also contains articles on individual plays. Quinn's earlier "Dickens as Shavian Metaphor" (*ShawR,* 1975) describes how "the fertile world of Dickens served Shaw as a vast garden from which to pluck the ready allusion, the illustrative witticism, the characteristic metaphor."

them in performance, the sharp edge that is present in almost everything that he did gets blunted." In "Bernard Shaw, Ibsen and the Ethics of English Socialism" (*VS,* 1978), I. M. Britain, like Wisenthal, attacks the misconception that Shaw treated Ibsen as a socialist or that Ibsen was indeed one. Shaw, Britain writes, recognized Ibsen's individualism and even used it to criticize socialist colleagues for their inflexibility. Alfred Turco's "*The Quintessence of Ibsenism*" (*TSLL,* 1976) examines the treatise for the consistency and cogency of its philosophy. "Shaw intuits," Turco concludes, "that the prospect of implementing his own reformist goals will depend upon an ability to resist grand designs foredoomed to failure by the nature of the world." Keith May's *Ibsen and Shaw* (1985) examines the *Quintessence* and compares playwriting strategies and theories, seeing Ibsen as essentially tragic and Shaw as comic. The Shavian position, May writes, "was that the human will alone can undo the errors of the intellect, *which are errors of the defeated will.* Perhaps they are, but Shaw never even glimpsed the true tragic position . . . that the will must always be exercised and fairly regularly defeated."

4

Biographies and Autobiographies

A diary is an autobiography of sorts, and Shaw made several stabs at keeping a diary. Shaw's Pitman shorthand diaries of 1885–97 (at the British Library of Political and Economic Science, familiarly the LSE) have long been quoted from incomplete transliterations made by Blanche Patch and Stanley Rypins. Other diary and early memoir fragments have been part of the BL Shaw archive in the British Museum. These have been gathered in *Bernard Shaw: The Diaries 1885–1897, with early autobiographical notebooks and diaries, and an abortive 1917 diary* (ed. S. Weintraub, 1986). The Rypins transliteration is the basis for the diary text, with additions and corrections by others versed in Shaw's Pitman. Annotations are coded to the Laurence *Bibliography*.

Written without view to publication and often laconic in the extreme, the *Diaries* are the key to the authentic early Shaw as well as a lens with which to examine "radical" intellectual life in the London of the 1880s and 1890s—how it was lived, what it cost to live it, how Shaw managed his multifarious pursuits of women, fortune, and fame. While many of Shaw's letters, even the earliest of them, evoke a writer already stage-managing a persona—part of their enduring charm—Shaw lays himself bare only in the day-to-day entries of the diary he soon failed to have time (or motive) to keep up.

Although Shaw never wrote an autobiography, he put vast segments of memoir material into his prefaces, pamphlets, essays, lectures, lay sermons, tracts, private letters, and other writings, collecting some of the autobiographical pieces with a few new essays in his *Sixteen Self Sketches* and in the process silently censoring or amending old articles and letters. Several of his prefaces were substantial contributions to the memoirs he would never write, particularly those to the novel *Immaturity* (written 1921) and *London Music in 1888–89* (written 1935). The *Sketches* and the two prefaces form the core of *Shaw: An Autobiography 1856–1898,* which, with its sequel (subtitled *The Playwright Years: 1898–1950*), both edited by S. Weintraub (1969, 1970), forms a continuous narrative by stitching together extracts from Shaw's autobiographical writings and concluding with Shaw's last will and testament.

The most comprehensive biography, Michael Holroyd's *Bernard Shaw,* authorized by the Shaw estate, gains its authority from the accessibility of the *Diaries* and thousands of Shaw letters, published and unpublished. The first volume, subtitled *The Search for Love* (1988), covers the years through Shaw's marriage in 1898; the second, *The Pursuit of Power* (1989), concludes in 1918 with the end of World War I; the third, *The Lure of Fantasy* (1991), spans the period of the political extravaganzas and completes the life. The three volumes, however, contain no source notes for Holroyd's documentation or his use of data first published by earlier researchers, except for some credits in the narrative itself. A fourth volume will survey GBS scholarship since Shaw's death in 1950, and publish notes to the three previous volumes.

Shaw contributed lavishly to biographical books about him done in his lifetime, thus furnishing them with a below-the-surface autobiographical dimension. He provided a young Irish-American scholar, T. D. O'Bolger, with hundreds of words of memoir detail for the updating of his dissertation, "The Real Shaw" (University of Pennsylvania, 1913), into a book, then prevented its publication. (The manuscript is at Harvard.) Prudently keeping copies of many letters to O'Bolger, Shaw eventually used the details himself, particularly for the preface to *Immaturity*. For Frank Harris, Shaw not only composed a Harrisian parody, "How Frank Would Have Done It," which appeared in his former editor's *Contemporary Portraits* (1919), but later helped complete a biography of himself of which Harris, at the end of his life, had managed only the first sixty-five pages. Privately Shaw considered it mostly his book, although Harris's paid ghostwriter, Frank Scully, computed the printed text of *Bernard Shaw* (1931) as seventy-two percent Scully (often through rewriting G.B.S.'s letters) and twenty-two percent Shaw (the remainder, apparently, Harris).

"How Frank Would Have Done It" was not the first of Shaw's autobiographical writings produced in the third person. Most of these were self-interviews purporting to record live and spontaneous give-and-take. Among the more elaborate third-person attempts, some of them serious efforts to control his history, others only elaborate private jokes, is the chapter (xxvii) Shaw wrote in November 1902 for Cyril Maude's *The Haymarket Theatre: Some Records and Reminiscences* (1903) describing the ill-fated rehearsals for a Maude production—which never came off—of Shaw's comedy *You Never Can Tell.* Forty years later Shaw spent months rewriting and adding to Hesketh Pearson's *G.B.S.* (1942), first making penciled corrections and interpolations that Pearson could rewrite and rub out and then writing red-inked comments meant for background rather than publication.

In Shaw's lifetime his biographers were often saddled with the autobiographer as collaborator. Authorized biographer Archibald Henderson had his first of three Shavian biographies held up while Shaw insisted that the book needed more work, some of which came from dozens of autobiographical letters that

Henderson turned largely into the third person. One (3–17 January 1905, in *Letters,* vol. 2) was more than twelve thousand words. Later biographers were also assisted by mail. Even into Shaw's nineties, as was the case with William Irvine, the biographee provided interlinear emendations for a typescript (chaps. 1 and 2 of *The Universe of G.B.S.,* 1949).

Most of the books about Shaw in the first three decades of the twentieth century were commentaries and elucidations, few of them with an substantial or reliable biographical data. The first major biography was Archibald Henderson's mammoth (and authorized) *George Bernard Shaw: His Life and Works* (1911), perhaps the largest such volume ever produced about a contemporary only halfway through his career. It was augmented by his *Bernard Shaw: Playboy and Prophet* (1932) and his *Bernard Shaw: Man of the Century* (1956), each indispensable for its detail (the three overlap, but later volumes necessarily cut back on earlier material) yet sometimes unreliable because Henderson—a mathematician by training—often uncritically accepted what Shaw gave him in such overwhelming profusion.

Frank Harris's *Bernard Shaw: An Unauthorized Biography* (1931) suffered from the handicaps of Harris's flair for sensation and Shaw's ostensible desire to supply it for the ailing and faltering biographer. Hesketh Pearson's *G.B.S.: A Full-Length Portrait* (1942), the text of which Shaw revised and augmented, was deliberately, in the Pearson manner, long on anecdote and short on documentation. William P. Cash's "What They Really Wrote about G.B.S.: Shaw and Pearson's 'Retreat to Moscow,' " *JML* (1986), demonstrates that Pearson's "Retreat to Moscow" chapter was written almost entirely by Shaw, presumably to put himself in a more favorable light than the original draft had done. After Shaw's death Pearson revised his book as *George Bernard Shaw: His Life and Personality* (1963), to include his *G.B.S.: A Postscript,* published immediately after Shaw's death in 1950 to capitalize on the event and to utilize material compiled since first publication and/or withheld from print as a matter of delicacy in Shaw's lifetime.

Also written in Shaw's lifetime were William Irvine's *The Universe of G.B.S.* (1949), still the standard account of Shaw's intellectual development; R. F. Rattray's handbook-chronology, *Bernard Shaw: A Chronicle* (1950); Shaw's secretary Blanche Patch's valuable sourcebook *Thirty Years with G.B.S.* (1951); and Stephen Winsten's *Days with Bernard Shaw* (1949). Winsten, once Shaw's Ayot St. Lawrence neighbor, also produced a second book of purported conversations, *Shaw's Corner* (1952), and *Jesting Apostle: The Life of Bernard Shaw* (1956); however, the factual dubiousness of the latter suggests that all three Winsten books should be used with caution.

An enlightening snippet by a Shaw contemporary, Sydney C. Cockerell, deserves a place in any biographical survey. "Shavian," *TLS* (29 July 1960), related a story told to Cockerell by William Morris in the early 1890s about Shaw finding the adjectival form of his surname in the encounter of a scholar named Shaw with a footnote referring to him followed by the Latin words *sic shavius sed inepte.* Amused, G.B.S. adopted the Latin form of his name.

Although the 1950s were too close to Shaw's passing for publication of studies not begun in his lifetime, in the anniversary year itself came two major full-length biographies. Henderson's *Man of the Century* (1956), while less readable than St. John Ervine's *Bernard Shaw: His Life, Work and Friends* (1956), is more reliable, since the Ervine book, although by an Irish biographer and playwright once personally close to Shaw, lacks not only documentation but also objectivity, warped as it is by the author's declared antipathies toward Fabianism and Shaw's many Fabian friends. A later, less ambitious biography, particularly useful with respect to Shaw's music-critic years but entirely leaning on standard sources, is Audrey Williamson's *Bernard Shaw: Man and Writer* (1963), while a gossipy and unreliable biographical source (rather than biography) is R. J. Minney's *Recollections of George Bernard Shaw* (1969). Other books in the decades since Shaw's death have been built on the author's authentic or indirect—or assumed—relationship to Shaw. Lawrence Langner of the Theatre Guild, for example, produced *G.B.S. and the Lunatic* (1963), largely a rehash, with augmentations, of his Shaw chapters in *The Magic Curtain* (1951); and Valerie Pascal Delacorte's *The Disciple and His Devil* (1970) concerned Shaw's film-director Gabriel Pascal, who brought *Pygmalion* and *Major Barbara* to the screen. Eileen O'Casey's third volume about herself and her husband, *Cheerio Titan: The Friendship between George Bernard Shaw and Eileen and Sean O'Casey* (1989) recycles earlier material and adds some newer memories and letters.

Other books by or about actors and directors and related theater people often depend heavily if not exclusively on the subject's relationship to Shaw—Rex Harrison (two books), Edith Evans, Raymond Massey, Cedric Hardwicke, Barry Jackson, Ralph Richardson, Alex Clunes, Marjorie Deans, Gertrude Lawrence, Margaret Webster, and Lillah McCarthy are examples that only suggest the potential in this genre.

Two books compiled by Allen Chappelow fall roughly into the same category. The first is *Shaw the Villager and Human Being: A Biographical Symposium* (1961), a collection of memoir pieces by Shaw's friends and neighbors emerging out of Chappelow's visits to Ayot St. Lawrence in 1950 to photograph Shaw. One of the photographs, showing the ninety-four-year-old G.B.S., walking stick in hand, Shaw christened "The Chucker-Out," thus giving Chappelow his title for a sequel volume. *Shaw—"The Chucker-Out"* (1969), misrepresented as the most detailed account available of Shaw's social, moral, and political views, is disabled by the editor's unreliable analyses but remains useful for its biographical source material—extracts from Shaw's speeches, provincial newspaper cuttings, and other pronouncements lifted from obscure locations. (Unfortunately few are fully transcribed, identified completely, or represented accurately.) A companion to Chappelow's earlier volume is Louise Rumball's *George Bernard Shaw and Ayot St. Lawrence: Memories and Facts by a Villager 1905–1930* (1987), which includes local color, photos, and G.B.S. postcards from the 1920s.

In the 1960s, with the beginnings of accessibility of archival material from the Shaw estate, biographical interest in Shaw increased strikingly. Stanley Weintraub's *Private Shaw and Public Shaw: A Dual Portrait of Lawrence of Arabia and G.B.S.* (1963) analyzes the intersecting lives of Shaw and the war hero who became his surrogate son over the period from their meeting in 1922 to "Shaw's" (T. E. changed his name legally in 1927) death in a motorcycle accident in 1935. Later, in another close biographical analysis of a crucial period in Shaw's life, *Journey to Heartbreak* (1971), S. Weintraub probes the war years 1914–18 and their aftermath for Shaw (*Heartbreak* is also useful with respect to the origins and development of *Back to Methuselah* and *Heartbreak House,* while *Private Shaw* has considerable detail on *Saint Joan* and on *Too True to Be Good,* in which "T. E. Shaw" is "Private Meek.") Also in the early 1960s came Janet Dunbar's *Mrs. G.B.S.* (1963), a biography of Charlotte Shaw that emphasized her strikingly unhappy although affluent childhood and premarital life (the Shaws married in their early forties in 1898) but scanted the years of her poor health and decline (1932–43).

Ample documentation now exists to appraise Shaw's earliest decades, which appear far more complex than Shaw's lighthearted view of them in his memoir writings. B. C. Rosset's seminal although overly sweeping *Shaw of Dublin: The Formative Years* (1964) is a massive exploration of Shaw's childhood, the ménage à trois in which it was largely lived, and its implications in Shaw's playwriting, while John O'Donovan's thin *Shaw and the Charlatan Genius* (1965) focuses on young Shaw's relationship with the interloper in the household, music teacher George John Vandeleur Lee. Paralleling this period although moving chronologically beyond it is Henry George Farmer's hostile *Bernard Shaw's Sister and Her Friends* (1959), which appears to possess the apparatus of genuine research but is primarily an ax-grinding polemic aimed at demonstrating that Shaw was jealous of his older sister Lucy, lacked affection for her, and kept her out of his life. Dan H. Laurence supplements the record of Shaw's formative years in "The [Edward] McNulty Memoir," about Shaw's earliest significant friendship, in *SHAW* 12 (1992). A largely superseded study of the years of apprenticeship, which defines the formative years as extending into Shaw's forties—J. Percy Smith's *The Unrepentant Pilgrim: A Study of the Development of Bernard Shaw* (1965)—utilizes BL and LSE archival material until then unavailable.

Few of Shaw's early friendships from his literary apprenticeship days in London are chronicled; however, one has been examined twice. Betty Hugo's "Very Innocent Epistles: the Letters of Elinor Huddart to Shaw" (*SHAW* 10, 1990) extracts from the BL Shaw archives to look at Shaw's largely epistolary relationship with the obscure novelist; and earlier, in J. Percy Smith's "Shaw's First Critic," *UTQ* (1971), an uninformatively titled essay that Hugo's overlaps, Smith emphasizes the pathos of Huddart's situation. The 1878–94 correspondence is one-sided: both critics must elicit G.B.S. from the letters of the sender, but the possibilities of the approach are rich and can be adapted to other one-way correspondences.

More journalism than biography is C.G.L. DuCann's *The Loves of George Bernard Shaw* (1963), which treats in separate Sunday-supplement chapters G.B.S.'s amorous (and other) relationships with the women in his life; yet even so it is more reliable than Tullah Hanley's *The Strange Triangle of G.B.S.* (1956), a "novel" based on the Shaw-Janet Achurch correspondence. Still another book about Shaw's relationship with a young woman is Peter Tompkins's cautious *Shaw and Molly Tompkins* (1961), about a Shavian effort to play Pygmalion (or Henry Higgins) toward an aspiring but untalented American actress in the 1920s and 1930s (C. A. Berst's long essay in *SHAW* 5 supersedes this); while Vincent Wall's small study, *Bernard Shaw: Pygmalion to Many Players* (1973), reviews G.B.S.'s activities as self-appointed mentor to actresses over two generations.

Other biographical books deal with Shaw's relationships with individuals crucial in his life. Arthur H. Nethercot's two-volume biography of Annie Besant, *The First Five Lives of Annie Besant* (1960) and *The Last Four Lives of Annie Besant* (1963), especially the first volume, examine one of the crucial female friendships of Shaw's early professional years. C. B. Purdom's *Harley Granville Barker* (1956), although a full life of the actor-director-playwright, derives much of its interest from Shaw's earliest relationship with a surrogate-son figure; Eric Salmon's *Granville Barker: A Secret Life* (1984) suggests unconvincingly, in a volume otherwise much superior to Purdom's, that Shaw was possibly Barker's illegitimate father; Margot Peters's *Mrs Pat* (1984) gains much of its interest from detailing Shaw's relationship with Mrs. Campbell; William B. Furlong's *GBS/GKC: Shaw and Chesterton: The Metaphysical Jesters* (1970) explores the interrelationships of the writer-debaters who were public enemies and private friends all their lives. Collecting (with revisions and augmentation) biographical essays published separately, S. Weintraub's *The Unexpected Shaw: Biographical Approaches to G.B.S. and His Work* (1982) examines unfamiliar backgrounds of major works and significant friendships (such as those with Sean O'Casey and Frank Harris) and looks at such less familiar aspects of the man as Shaw the actor, Shaw the boxer, Shaw the art critic and literary critic, and Shaw the emergent Irish patriot. Michael Holroyd's *The Genius of Shaw* (1979) contains essays by many hands, a number of them biographical: "The First Twenty Years," by John O'Donovan; "In the Picture Galleries," by S. Weintraub; "The Way of No Flesh," by Brigid Brophy; "The Fabian Ethic," by Robert Skidelsky; "Women and the Body Politic," by M. Holroyd; "As Lonely as God," by M. Peters; and "Man of Letters," by Barbara Smoker. Best among Holroyd's own occasional biographical pieces on Shaw is "Shaw at Shaw's Corner" in the National Trust's *Writers at Home* (1985), which richly evokes the texture of the Shaws' life in their tiny Hertfordshire village.

The "way of no flesh" is the subject, also, of *The George Bernard Shaw Vegetarian Cook Book*, ed. Alice Laden—Shaw's housekeeper-cook 1943–1950—and R. J. Minney (1971). A recipe book of Shaw's favorites, it is heavy on lentils, vegetables, and sugary desserts.

Almost an autobiography is *Shaw: An Exhibit* (ed. Dan H. Laurence, 1978), the catalog of the exhibition at the Humanities

Research Center at the University of Texas, Austin, which exemplifies Shaw's life through quotation, illustration, and facsimile samples of Shaw documentation from his earliest years to his death, the last item being Shaw's death mask (only described). The death mask itself has been reproduced as a frontispiece (*CVE*, no. 9–10, 1979). Laurence's monograph *Shaw, Books and Libraries* (1976) is an informal account of Shaw's attitudes toward letters, manuscripts, books, and book production and his public spiritedness toward libraries and the book trade in general.

A hybrid biography/autobiography, *Shaw: Interviews and Recollections*, ed. A. M. Gibbs (1990), brings together Shavian interviews and self-interviews as well as a myriad of reminiscences, all grouped under such categories as "Growing Up," "Fabian Socialist and Platform Speaker," "Plays and Players," "Philanderer and Married Man," and "Old Age and Death." One section, "World Travels," in effect supplements an earlier book. A collective biography of the public man, *SHAW* 5, *Shaw Abroad* (ed. Rodelle Weintraub, 1985), illuminates Shaw's experiences in, and the literary impact upon him of, Germany (John J. Weisert); 1890s Italy (E. B. Adams); Sweden (Ishrat Lindblad); Jamaica (S. Weintraub); Ireland (N. Grene); France (J. C. Amalric); post-1920 Italy (C. A. Berst); Yugoslavia (Damir Kalogjera); Soviet Russia (T. F. Evans); South Africa (Leon H. Hugo); India (Valli Rao); Hong Kong and China (Piers Gray); Japan (Sidney Albert and Junko Matoba); America (Dan H. Laurence), with a Hollywood afterword (B. F. Dukore); and New Zealand (Murray Martin); with a Shaw travel piece on Switzerland, and two Holy Land interviews. A different biographical perspective appears in M. Peters's *Bernard Shaw and the Actresses* (1980), which examines Shaw's relations with actresses and nonactresses alike, beginning with Alice Lockett and Jenny Patterson (a particularly illuminating section) and concluding with Molly Tompkins. Other feminine perspectives are two biographical articles by R. Weintraub that focus on Charlotte Shaw: "Shaw's Celibate Marriage: Its Impact on His Plays" (*CVE*, 1979) and "The Irish Lady in Shaw's Plays" (*ShawR*, 1980). A further look at Shavian real-life models for his characters is found in William Amos, *The Originals: An A–Z of Fiction's Real-Life Characters* (1985), which examines nearly fifty of Shaw's creations from previously published sources, the results ranging from obvious to farfetched.

Of genealogical and perhaps biographical value is Nathaniel Harris's *The Shaws: The Family of George Bernard Shaw* (1977). Charles Macmahon Shaw's *Bernard's Brethren* (1939), by an Australian offshoot of the large Shaw family, is a memoir enlivened by G.B.S.'s corrections of his cousin's account in red ink (typeface) on opposing pages, the book's major interest. While Charles recalls meeting G.B.S. in Dublin in 1871 as a boy, G.B.S. accepts only that they met in the 1930s "as ancient men."

Of biographical and critical interest is Arnold Silver's *Bernard Shaw: The Darker Side* (1982), which examines Shaw and his work from a largely pathological and Freudian perspective, seeing Shaw's humanity as disabled by oedipal and related psychological disturbances. A mordant and suspicious viewer of Shaw's motives and creative inspiration in lengthy analyses of several plays, in particular *The Simpleton of the Unexpected Isles, Candida, Man and Superman,* and *Pygmalion,* Silver sees sadistic and even homicidal tendencies in Shaw emerging from unresolved oedipal dilemmas. Conversely, there are many articles on Shaw's passion, humanity, and generosity, notable among them Jacques Barzun's warm "Eros, Priapos, and Shaw," in *The Play and Its Critic: Essays for Eric Bentley* (ed. Michael Bertin, 1986), which explodes the fallacy among critics of Shaw "that because one cares about ideas one cannot care also about people."

Articles with a biographical basis include Mavor Moore's "Why 'James Mavor' Morell?" (*ShawR*, 1980), about the Scot economist James Mavor; S. Weintraub's "Bernard Shaw and 'The Unknown Soldier' " (*TLS*, November 1981), about what Shaw called a scenario for an antiwar play; and Weintraub's "Shaw's Other Keegan: Sean O'Casey and G.B.S.," in *Sean O'Casey Centenary Essays* (ed. R. R. Lowery and David Krause, 1980). Mary O'Connor's "Did Bernard Shaw Kill John Davidson? The 'Tragi-comedy' of a Commissioned Play" (*ShawR*, 1978) details Shaw's unsuccessful attempt to revive the Edwardian poet's literary fortunes by financing a work, *The Game of Life*, that would not be a potboiler; the result was, ironically, frustration and suicide. Dealing with the same period in Shaw's life, Annie Russell's "George Bernard Shaw at Rehearsals of *Major Barbara*" (*ShawR*, 1976) is a 1908 account by the first English Barbara, once delivered by her as a lecture; it includes letters from Shaw to her and to Louis Calvert, the play's first Undershaft. Shaw as publicist is the subject of Dan H. Laurence's "What's Your Opinion, Mr Shaw?" (*LCUT*, 1974), which details Shaw's relationships with interviewers and would-be interviewers who besieged him for his views on practically everything.

Books with major sections on Shaw also contribute to the biographical picture. Although the availability of Shaw's 1885–94 *Diaries* now vastly enlarges the range of detail, the fullest analysis of Shaw's cart-and trumpet role outside the full-length lives remains "George Bernard Shaw: Rhetorician and Public Speaker" by Marie Hochmuth Nichols, in her *Rhetoric and Criticism* (1963). Stanley Pierson's *British Socialists: The Journey from Fantasy to Politics* (1979) examines the transition in the focus of Shaw's plays, from narrow and specific to general and universal, beginning at a time when his socialist activities still involved concern over public lavatories and the municipalization of utilities. Shaw realized that a drama controlled by socialist preoccupations was too limited, and he began, while still immersed in Fabian politics, to explore human behavior in a way that went beyond promoting a socialist reorganization of society. Shaw's futuristic plays would recognize that a better world required better human beings more than idealistic legislation. David I. Rabey's *British and Irish Political Drama in the Twentieth Century: Implicating the Audience* (1986) includes a chapter entitled "Socialist Supermen and Pilgrim's Progress." More specifically, *Shaw and Politics* (*Shaw* 11, 1991), ed. T. F. Evans, covers the gamut of Shaw's political activities from his early days in London to his last.

Another aspect of Shaw appears in Benny Green's *Shaw's*

Champions: G.B.S. and Prizefighting from Cashel Byron to Gene Tunney (1978), which is augmented by S. Weintraub's "A Passion for Pugilism" (*TLS*, 5 May 1978), an essay itself augmented in his *Unexpected Shaw*. Diana Farr's *Gilbert Cannan: A Georgian Prodigy* (1978), a book about the then-young critic and playwright whom G.B.S. caricatured as "Gilbert Gunn" in *Fanny's First Play*, has a chapter on Shaw. Jeffrey Meyers's *Married to Genius* (1977) reviews the Shaw marriage, which Meyers considers a "muffinlike" marriage of convenience that left both parties discontented. George Hendrick's *Henry Salt: Humanitarian Reformer and Man of Letters* (1977) details Shaw's nonsexual involvement in the nonsexual marriage of Henry Salt and his lesbian wife, Kate. Yvonne Kapp's *Eleanor Marx* (2 vols., 1976) chronicles Shaw's involvement with both Eleanor Marx and the unscrupulous Edward Aveling (one of the originals for Louis Dubedat in *The Doctor's Dilemma*) in their clearly heterosexual nonmarriage. Also valuable for its picture of the rising Shaw of the 1880s and 1890s is Julia Briggs's *A Woman of Passion: The Life of E. Nesbit, 1858–1924* (1987), whose amorous interest in G.B.S. is detailed in the *Diaries* and fictionalized in *An Unfinished Novel* (1958; see preface by S. Weintraub). Autobiographical elements in the plays abound, and many references to them will be found under individual plays in Chapter 9 and in the biographies of Shaw.

Victor Bonham-Carter's *Authors by Profession* (2 vols., 1978 and 1984) devotes chapters to Shaw's relationship with the Society of Authors, his methods of publishing, and his opposition to stage censorship. Joseph R. Dunlap's "The Typographical Shaw" (*Shavian*, 1961) examines Shaw's role at the turn of the century in the Morris-inspired revival of printing. Norman MacKenzie and Jeanne MacKenzie's *The Fabians* (1977), more accurately entitled *The First Fabians* in the London edition, provides a detailed account of the Fabian Society from 1883 to 1914 and necessarily includes much on G.B.S. the politician and amateur economist. N. MacKenzie's edition of *The Letters of Sidney and Beatrice Webb* (3 vols., 1978) includes many letters to Shaw and helps further to place him in the Fabian movement as well as in the context of his friendship with the Webbs. Even more valuable is the MacKenzies' four-volume edition of *The Diary of Beatrice Webb* (1982–86), which is replete with vignettes and observations about Shaw, ranging from hostile to grudgingly admiring, penned by a witness to much of his career (she died in 1943) who envied his success and deplored his lack of Webbian socialist seriousness. (The complete diary, much of it still unpublished, is at the LSE.)

Hardly less valuable among collections of letters *to* Shaw is chapter 3 of Eric Salmon's edition of *Granville Barker and His Correspondents* (1986), which publishes texts of nearly fifty letters and postcards, 1900–1943, from Barker to Shaw. These complement nearly 150 from Shaw's side published by C. B. Purdom in *Bernard Shaw's Letters to Granville Barker* (1956), and those in the Laurence edition.

Shaw's interest in and use of psychology is explored by Sidney Albert (*MD*, 1971), who augments and corrects A. H. Nethercot (*MD*, 1969). Daniel Dervin's *Bernard Shaw: A Psychological Study* (1975) attempts a book-length analysis of Shaw's psychology. Predecessor studies are few, notably Philip Weissman's chapter, "Shaw's Childhood and *Pygmalion*," in *Creativity in the Theater: A Psychoanalytic Study* (1965), and Erik H. Erikson's "The Problem of Ego Identity" (*Journal of the American Psychoanalytical Association*, 1956), which incautiously takes Shaw's tales about his childhood in the prefaces to *Immaturity* and *London Music* at face value. Shaw's psychological interests, and in particular his interest in dreams, continue to be explored, as in R. Weintraub's "Johnny's Dream: *Misalliance*" (*SHAW* 7, 1987), which examines what Barbara Watson has labeled "Shaw's literary parallel to Freudianism." (For both *Misalliance* and *Heartbreak House* as dreams, see discussions of these plays.)

5

EARLY CRITICISM

In his introduction to the first of what would be a flood of books, American journalist H. L. Mencken wrote (in *George Bernard Shaw: His Plays*, 1905), "Pick up any of the literary monthlies and you will find a disquisition upon his technique, glance through the dramatic column of your favorite newspaper and you will find some reference to his plays." By assiduous self-advertisement as well as by the apparent novelty of his plays, Shaw had begun to be written about in the periodical press; however, Mencken's book—the first entirely on Shaw—appeared only in Shaw's fiftieth year. (The table of contents of Mencken's study advertised chapters on the novels and on the major plays from *Widowers' Houses* to *Major Barbara*, but no chapter on the latter play was printed.) Holbrook Jackson's *Bernard Shaw* (1907), the first G.B.S. study to be published in England, emphasized the playwright as "a leader of thought," the integrator of philosophy and drama, and compared him in relation to his era with Swift and Carlyle. In the same year appeared Desmond MacCarthy's *The Court Theatre*, a review of the 1904–7 seasons at the

Court under the management of J. E. Vedrenne and Harley Granville Barker. Of the 988 performances, 701 were of eleven Shaw plays. MacCarthy's criticism, insisting that Shaw's plays aimed at forcing men to examine their pretensions, their emotions, and their consciences, stands up well in its scrutiny of the plays' theatrical values, with his review of *Major Barbara* still one of the best analyses of that complex work. MacCarthy's *Shaw* (1950) collects all of his reviews of Shaw's plays he wished to preserve.

Another early study that remains useful, although ideologically hostile to Shaw, is G. K. Chesterton's still provocative *George Bernard Shaw* (1909; enlarged 1935). While Chesterton praised Shaw's gaiety and wit he deplored his extravagantly "heartless" view of human relations, which meant that it failed to coincide with G.K.C.'s conservative near-medievalism. On the continent two books on Shaw appeared before the war, in opposing camps. Augustin Hamon, French translator of Shaw's plays, produced the admiring *Le Molière du xxe siècle: Bernard Shaw* (1913, English trans. 1916); H. Richter, in Leipzig, published "Die Quintessenz des Shawismus" (*EngS,* 1913). A final prewar book, Joseph McCabe's *George Bernard Shaw* (1914), was, in its author's view, "a critical interpretation of the man and his message" and an overt, rationalist response to Chesterton's strictures. For a survey of the range of pre-1914 critical opinion, the T. F. Evans *Critical Heritage* volume (1976) is valuable.

In the journals, the best prewar writing on Shaw was that of a young critic who would be a war casualty, Dixon Scott. His *Bookman* article (1913) was a balanced appraisal of Shaw's dramatic method ("the tyranny of technique over temperament") and prose style ("one of the most remarkable verbal weapons ever forged . . . , an instrument built expressly for cut-and thrust platform work"). More than any other critic of his time, Scott probed intelligently into Shaw's shortcomings as a dramatist yet concluded that "once the [traditional] limitations of the plays are realized they cease to possess any," recognizing that the force propelling his dramatic prose was "a passion for purity, gentleness, truth, justice and beauty." In 1916 Scott's essay reappeared in a posthumous collection of his essays, *Men of Letters,* by which time John Palmer had published a long article in the *Fortnightly Review* (1915), "Bernard Shaw: An Epitaph." With the outbreak of war, and Shaw's unpopular points of view regarding it, it was fashionable to consider Shaw's influence on the wane—thus the title—yet Palmer continued to give Shaw high marks, foreshadowing the change in public opinon that would recognize Shaw as sage by war's end. (The transition is the narrative thread in S. Weintraub's *Journey to Heartbreak.*)

Three book-length wartime critical studies were less than fully admiring. Harold Owen's *Common Sense about the Shaw* (1915) hysterically attacked *Common Sense about the War* and G.B.S. in general; in *Bernard Shaw: A Critical Study* (1915), Percival P. Howe castigated the "publicist's unreality" of Shaw's plays, the product of a view of life limited to "the Fabian Society and the cart and trumpet"; and in *Bernard Shaw: The Man and the Mask* (1916), Richard Burton saw a theatrical sensibility beyond capability of any other contemporary but also an ambivalence which left him suspicious of overt meanings in Shaw. Most writing about Shaw during the war, his most unpopular period, suggests that books about him would have been a hazardous commercial enterprise in 1914–18. Newspaper attacks were frequent and emotional. Considered opinion largely awaited the release of his new plays, products of a war that had inhibited major dramatic statement.

The publication of *Heartbreak House* (1919) and *Back to Methuselah* (1921) did little at the time to advance Shaw's reputation, nor did their performances, although both works, particularly the former, have gained respect in time through performance and later criticism. As Graham Sutton observed in *The Bookman* in 1924, Shaw's detractors often based their arguments on mutually exclusive points of view: "Half of them complain that Mr. Shaw is too serious, the other half that he is not serious enough." Performances (New York, 1923; London, 1924) of *Saint Joan* reversed the direction of criticism, the public (with critics rushing to follow) seeing the play as a contemporary classic. The Nobel Prize for Literature came in 1926; a few years later Winston Churchill referred to Shaw in *Great Contemporaries* as "the greatest living master of letters in the English-speaking world." Shaw's later plays (written once he was past seventy) showed an inevitable weakening of his dramaturgical hand, and his cranky political views as a new war approached were unpopular. Nevertheless, criticism thereafter largely accepted the premise that he was the most significant English playwright since Shakespeare as well as a master at many of the other literary trades. In his last full decade, the 1940s, his ninetieth birthday and its aftermath precipitated a shelf of books and other studies, from biographies and memoirs to works of substantial criticism. A number of these remain among the most lasting contributions to an understanding of the man and his work.

6

General Critical Evaluations

Once the Shavian canon was relatively established in the late 1940s, the first real flowering of criticism followed. Eric Bentley succeeded his discussions of *Candida* and other early plays in *The Playwright as Thinker* (1946) with *Shaw: A Reconsideration* (1947; rev. 1957 as *Bernard Shaw*), still useful particularly for its analyses of the "newness" in Shaw's dramaturgy. William Irvine's *The Universe of G.B.S.* (1949) benefited from Shaw's own reading of the text and remains a solid foundation for the study of the ideas in Shaw's plays and his general intellectual development as a child of Victorian radicalism. Similar in intent, but structured about particular Victorian concepts, is Julian B. Kaye's *Bernard Shaw and the Nineteenth-Century Tradition* (1958), its approach identifiable from such chapter headings as "The Rebellion against Mid-Century Mechanism" and "Shaw and Nineteenth-Century Political Economists." Also probing Shaw's cultural inheritance, but from the perspective of popular drama rather than ideas, is Martin Meisel's *Shaw and the Nineteenth-Century Theatre* (1963), which relates Shaw's playwriting techniques and subjects to his experience, as spectator and drama critic, of Victorian dramatic genres and their conventions of character, action, and setting.

A different conceptual approach to the canon is taken in A. H. Nethercot's *Men and Supermen: The Shavian Portrait Gallery* (1954; rev. 1966), which examines and classifies Shaw's characters first from the standpoint of Shaw's *Quintessence of Ibsenism* division of people into Philistine, Idealist, and Realist and then by occupation, sex, race, and aspiration. The *Theatrical Companion to Shaw* (ed. Raymond Mander and Joe Mitchenson, 1955) surveys the plays as performances, with photographs, lists of casts, plot summaries, sketchy extracts from early reviews, and valuable reprintings of Shavian program notes. (The program notes, supplemented by additional such notes, reappear in the Bodley Head Bernard Shaw.) A substantial shelf of general critical evaluations of the plays in book form exists, some of the volumes focused (at least titularly) on a thesis and some restricted to particular segments of the canon. Thus Arland Ussher's pungent *Three Great Irishmen: Shaw, Yeats, Joyce* (1952) looks at G.B.S.'s Irishness and, going beneath the sod, sees a Socrates who was also an Aristophanes. Restricted in another sense, Charles A. Carpenter, Jr., in *Bernard Shaw and the Art of Destroying Ideals* (1969), is concerned with the plays through *Man and Superman* and their dramatic strategies, which the critic sees as the destruction of audience delusions and preconceptions, leading (Shaw hoped) to popular reassessment of personal and societal values. J. L. Wisenthal's *The Marriage of Contraries* (1974) begins with *Man and Superman* and concludes with the first postwar plays, demonstrating Shaw's dramatic use of the tension (and often, then, the harmony) of opposites. C. A. Berst, scrutinizing the texts of ten major plays from *Mrs Warren* to *Saint Joan* (but not *Methuselah*) in *Bernard Shaw and the Art of Drama* (1973), a collection of essays referred to below under individual plays, explores Shaw's "complex and penetrating aesthetic sensibility." L. Crompton's *Shaw the Dramatist* (1969), the most intellectually based of the general books, examines twelve major plays through

Saint Joan from the standpoint of their social, philosophical, and historical backgrounds—and thus becomes a source for study of Shaw's themes, characters, and situations, Crompton relying for his clues not only upon internal and secondary evidence but and the examination of Shaw's extant play manuscripts. Another volume that uses the manuscripts to examine the plays is B. F. Dukore's *Bernard Shaw, Playwright* (1973), which probes Shaw's theory and practice as a playwright, often by studying his revisions and his intentions as seen in his published prefaces and private letters. M. Morgan, in an uneven but often insightful book, *The Shavian Playground* (1972), will be referred to play-by-play in appropriate places. Colin Wilson's confessedly "existential" *Bernard Shaw: A Reassessment* (1969) is illuminated by flashes of insight but handicapped by Wilson's all-encompassing, scriptural dedication to Shaw's Creative Evolution concepts. "I see him," Wilson insists of Shaw, "as an *evolutionary* portent." Homer Woodbridge's posthumous *G. B. Shaw: Creative Artist* (1963) is a series of apparently unrefurbished classroom lectures; and L. H. Hugo's *Bernard Shaw: Playwright and Preacher* (1971), is a general review of Shaw's thought in his plays. Hugo's somewhat skeptical view is a useful corrective and sets a tone for later survey books. Using a different theoretical approach, C. D. Sidhu in *The Pattern of Tragicomedy in Bernard Shaw* (1978) sees Shaw's comedy as a combination of "two distinct strains: the native [English] tradition of the mixture of laughter and tears, and the continuous Ibsenite undercurrent of the tragic inherent in the world-view presented." Maurice Valency's *The Cart and the Trumpet: The Plays of George Bernard Shaw* (1973) is a sound play-by-play examination of the canon, based on Valency's experiences as play translator and critic of European drama. Thus he brings to a view of Shaw his study of the late nineteenth-century philosophers and literary experimentalists, and he attempts (intriguingly yet not always convincingly) to see Shaw as Symbolist and to discover his relations—as Symbolist—with Strindberg, Wagner, Mallarmé, and other continental influences.

Special journal issues worth mention include the *New Edin-*

burgh Review (1975), which devoted two monthly issues to general essays on aspects of Shaw: *The Celebrated Buffoon* and *The Spring Heel'd Marcher*. "Shaw and Myth" (*ShawR*, ed. Timothy Vesonder, 1978), offers both an annotated checklist of research of Shaw from that perspective and articles described below under individual plays. Perhaps also in the category of Shaw and myth are Arthur Ganz's "The Playwright as Perfect Wagnerite: Motifs from the Music Dramas in the Theatre of Bernard Shaw" (*CD* 1979), and its sequel, Robert Coskren's "Wagner and Shaw: *Rheingold* Motifs in *Major Barbara*" (*CD*, 1980). Ganz examines how the myths in Wagner's transmutation apparently influenced *Candida, Caesar and Cleopatra, Man and Superman*, and *Major Barbara*, among others, and Coskren supplements the evidences of that impact on *Barbara*.

"Shaw around the World" (*ShawR*, 1977) furnishes performance histories of G.B.S. in Sweden, Norway, the Netherlands, France, Portugal, and Japan; I. Lindblad's article on Sweden, by giving details on Shaw's vicissitudes with the Nobel Prize committee, adds to Shavian biography as well. Two other articles concerned with performances are by Barbara Small (both in *ShawR*, 1979). The performance qualities as well as the performance problems in need of solution in Shaw's work for the theater are analyzed from the standpoint of voice in her "Rhetorical Style in Shaw's Plays," which points out the need to master the rhetorical style inherent in even the early plays despite their surface realism, and in "Shaw on Standard Stage Speech," which concerns the requirement for precise stage pronunciation despite the actor's need to be "something of a virtuoso in speech" and to have the ability "to assume dialects and drop or change them at will."

SHAW 1, Shaw and Religion (ed. C. A. Berst, 1981), includes an extensive annotated checklist: "Shaw and Religion/Philosophy," compiled by C. A. Carpenter; and early Shaw "sermon," "Some Necessary Repairs to Religion"; Berst's examination of Shaw's groping toward godhead in the nineties, "The Poetic Genesis of Shaw's God"; and essays noted under individual works. *SHAW* 3,

Shaw's Plays in Performance (ed. D. J. Leary, 1983) examines the range Shaw's plays and playwriting strategies from the standpoint of their performance values, with emphasis by individual critics on *Major Barbara* and *Pygmalion* and on the importance of setting and "Shavian" acting and direction. *SHAW* 5, *Shaw Abroad* (ed. R. Weintraub, 1985), has been referred to earlier as in effect a biography of the public man, but it also is informative on the relation of place to plays and details Shaw's encounters with France, Germany, Italy, China/Hong Kong, Japan, Russia, the United States, South Africa, India, New Zealand, Ireland (as tourist), Jamaica, the Holy Land, and Yugoslavia. *SHAW* 7, *Shaw: the Neglected Plays* (ed. Alfred Turco, Jr., 1987) examines such works as *The Philanderer, Fanny's First Play, John Bull's Other Island, Misalliance, Apple Cart,* and *Good King Charles*. Other such volumes are referred to in appropriate subject areas.

A number of companions to Shaw furnish general information, among them Michael and Mollie Hardwick's guide, *The Bernard Shaw Companion* (1973), Phyllis Hartnoll's annotated dramatis personae, *Who's Who in Shaw* (1975), and M. Morgan's *File on Shaw* (1989), which includes performance histories, summaries of and excerpts from reviews, and a chronology of Shaw's life and published writings. Short accounts vary so widely in quality that such pamphlets are noted only to be dismissed as dated (Ward, 1951, and some later revisions) or unreliable (Matthews, 1969); however, the sixty-five pages in J.I.M. Stewart's Oxford History of English Literature volume, *Eight Modern Writers* (1963), are incisive, insightful, unidolatrous criticism. The Twayne series includes a *George Bernard Shaw* (1978) by Eldon C. Hill, which follows the series format with chronology, biographical-critical chapters on the plays, and selected bibliography. Less successful as an introduction is Pat M. Carr's *Bernard Shaw* (1976) in the World Dramatists series, which is flawed by omissions and errors and is written at a level suggesting a secondary-school audience. Another brief survey volume is J. O'Donovan's *Bernard Shaw* (1983), largely spillover from his earlier *Charlatan Genius* with the last five decades rapidly treated.

Suffused with Irish moralism, it possesses an anachronistic charm that enables the reader to understand what Shaw escaped. Brief book-length general analyses of Shaw, particularly the plays, are a continuing phenomenon. A. M. Gibbs's *The Art and Mind of Shaw* (1983), A. Ganz's *George Bernard Shaw* (1983), and N. Grene's *Bernard Shaw: A Critical View* (1984) all are part of publishers' series, with the space drawbacks of such Procrustean limitations. Some major plays are thus completely ignored. Yet each study represents a healthy objectivity, offering no excuses for Shavian failings where they are perceived. Similarly, John A. Bertolini's *The Playwrighting Self of Bernard Shaw* (1991) deals with only six plays and some one-acters, focusing on details of language and subtleties of thought. Several chapters are noted under individual titles.

A many-sided examination of Shaw's principles and practice regarding feminism and feminist issues is *Fabian Feminist: Bernard Shaw and Woman* (ed. R. Weintraub, 1977). Although it concludes by reprinting five little-known Shavian polemics on woman suffrage, including a sardonic condemnation of forced feeding, and a checklist of works by and about Shaw that have a feminist perspective (comp. Lucile Kelling Henderson), the core of the book consists of essays grouped around the topics "Literary and Mythic Influences," "Political and Economic Influences," "Shaw's Liberated Woman," and "Influence of Shaw's Feminism." Also written from a feminist perspective is E. B. Adams's "Shaw's Ladies" (*ShawR*, 1980), on his use of "lady" not as a substitute for "woman," but as a "class marker"—as when Lina in *Misalliance* claims her independence (as a "person") and identifies herself as a "woman"—something that Hypatia understands but that the class-rigid men do not. (Possibly the most extreme denunciation of Shaw by a feminist has come from Germaine Greer in "A Whore in Every Home," her program essay for the National Theatre, London, production of *Mrs Warren's Profession*, which indicts Shaw for using as his example of the "profession" a competent and successful businesswoman rather than one of the far more numerous women brutalized by poverty and by her trade. "Whore" is included in *Fabian Feminist.*) Barbara B. Watson's *A Shavian Guide to the Intelligent Woman* (1964) is the pioneering feminist work, but additional critiques from a female perspective are burgeoning. An example from Sweden is Sonja Lorichs's *The Unwomanly Woman in Bernard Shaw's Drama and Her Social and Political Background* (1973). Many dissertations since pick up these themes.

Other book-length studies of the plays have, even more confessedly, special critical axes to grind and sometimes succeed in enlarging our perspectives. J. L. Wisenthal's *Shaw's Sense of History* (1988) is an example, examining Shavian plays with a historical texture through the lens of what proves to be Shaw's very considerable self-taught historical learning. We see, as J. B. Kaye demonstrated earlier in *Shaw and the Nineteenth-Century Tradition*, although with less specificity than Wisenthal, how Shaw responded in his plays to the historical insights of such Victorians as Carlyle, Macaulay, Buckle (often neglected in this context), and Ruskin. But Karl Marx was also a Victorian-era historian, and, less persuasively, Paul A. Hummert's *Bernard Shaw's Marxian Romance* (1973) sees Marx in almost every Shavian play and loses credibility in overstatement; yet many plays become better understood in the light of the Marxian grip upon Shaw, which slackened at times but never lifted. The grip of the Aesthetic Movement, particularly that of the Pre-Raphaelites (Shaw called *Candida* his Pre-Raphaelite play), is scrutinized throughout the canon in E. B. Adams's *Bernard Shaw and the Aesthetes* (1971), which is especially thorough on Shaw's views on art and artists in his plays. The interaction of nineteenth-century ideas and movements in Shaw's plays remains a fertile area for critics, as beneath the surface of Shavian drama is a battlefield of conflicting and overlapping Victorian ideologies often transformed by later twentieth-century experience.

S. P. Albert's "Bernard Shaw, Philosopher" (*JAAC*, 1956) remains the best of the short synthesizing studies from that angle; and there is a slender book by R. N. Roy, *Shaw's Philosophy of Life* (1964), which is an overview of the backgrounds of Shaw's thought. Although Roy acknowledges indebtedness to such earlier work as his compatroit S. C. Sen Gupta's *The Art of Bernard Shaw* (1950) and to C.E.M. Joad's *Shaw* (1949), Joad's reputation has diminished and his work on Shaw, however admiring, is largely discredited. Immature in thought as well as juvenile chronologically is Shaw's first prose work, *My Dear Dorothea*, written in 1878 before he was twenty-two, but unpublished until 1956 (ed. S. Winsten). Only about 4,200 words, it is subtitled ambitiously *A Practical System of Moral Education for Females* and covers behavior from at least *A* (advice-giving) to *V* (vanity). Few critics refer to it, and fewer biographers. Holroyd awards it a page, noting that Shaw had read *Lady Chesterfield's Letters to Her Daughter* a year earlier, and that by comparison Shaw's equivalent is "a damp squib." The only separate study is Laura Tahir's "*My Dear Dorothea:* Shaw's Earliest Sketch," *SHAW* 9 (1989), based upon an examination of the MS at Texas. Her conclusion is that it was a means by which Shaw came, early, "to deal with his anger toward authority figures" and that it "laid the foundation of his life's purpose," incubating ideas to be reworked over a long productive life.

Also taking a philosophical slant, and more successfully, is R. F. Whitman's provocative *Shaw and the Play of Ideas* (1977), which analyzes Shaw's intellectual development by stressing the impact—largely indirect, through E. Belfort Bax—of Hegel on the plays. Also philosophical in approach is *Shaw's Moral Vision: The Self and Salvation* (1976) by A. Turco, who examines Shaw's pragmatism as it emerges from the major critical essays of the 1890s, *The Quintessence of Ibsenism* and *The Perfect Wagnerite*, and moves onstage, culminating in *Major Barbara* and *Heartbreak House*. The most thorough examination of Shaw's impact on the philosophy of Henri Bergson, or, conversely, of Bergson on Shaw, is Michel Pharand's "Shaw's Life Force and Bergson's *Elan Vital*: a Question of Influence," *CVE* (April 1991), in which the verdict is no appreciable influence in either direction, but similar worldviews ascribed by Bergson himself to a confluence of thinking in which both were part of the same "mouvement d'idées."

Other books that concern Shaw's religious concepts and their background are Anthony S. Abbott's *Shaw and Christianity* (1965), Samuel A. Yorks's *The Evolution of Bernard Shaw* (1981), and W. S. Smith's *The Bishop of Everywhere* (1982). While Smith is more biographical and Yorks more critical, both offer approaches to Shaw's ideas about what he labeled Creative Evolution. A provocative study that identifies Shaw as part of a philosophical tradition that has speculated on the role of Will in evolution is Daniel J. Leary's "The Evolutionary Dialectic of Shaw and Teilhard [de Chardin]: A Perennial Philosophy" (*ShawR*, 1966). Also taking up the striking Teilhard parallels is W. S. Smith in "The Life Force, the Noosphere, and the New Religions" in his *The Bishop of Everywhere*.

An idiosyncratic study of Shaw as religious prophet is Colin Wilson's *Bernard Shaw: A Reassessment* (1969), but the least trustworthy of all such studies is the earlier C.E.M. Joad *Shaw* (1949), which cribs in haste from a variety of unacknowledged sources, particularly Dixon Scott. (See Julian Ross's "A Piece of Literary Shoplifting," *ShawR*, 1968.) Religious perspectives toward the canon are utilized by Gerald Weales in a survey chapter in *Religion in Modern British Drama* (1961) and—in dealing with Shaw as existential thinker—in B. F. Dukore's *Bernard Shaw, Playwright* (1973), and in entire books in A. Abbott's *Shaw and Christianity* (1965) and Alan Barr's *Victorian Stage Pulpiteer: Bernard Shaw's Crusade* (1973). The best work on Shaw as a religious thinker is by W. S. Smith. Preceding *The Bishop of Everywhere* were his two anthologies of Shavian writings (some previously unpublished), *The Religious Speeches of Bernard Shaw* (1963) and *Shaw on Religion* (1967), and most notably the much underrated *The London Heretics 1870–1914* (1968), which definitively examines liberal religious movements in London in late Victorian and Edwardian London, Shaw's influential role in them, and their influence upon Shaw's thinking and writing.

Book-length collections of general Shavian criticism by several hands are relatively few. S. Winsten's *G.B.S. 90: Aspects of Bernard Shaw's Life and Work* (1946) was the only one to appear in his lifetime and was of uneven critical value although of enduring value biographically for its recollections by G.B.S.'s contemporaries. R. J. Kaufmann's *G. B. Shaw: A Collection of Critical Essays* (1965) collects articles and essays of a more scholarly nature than most included in Louis Kronenberger's earlier volume, *George Bernard Shaw: A Critical Survey* (1953), largely a compilation of high-level journalism. (Holroyd's parallel volume was noted under Biography.) Harold Bloom's *George Bernard Shaw: Modern Critical Views* (1987) is distinguished by an idiosyncratically belligerent preface at odds with every essay collected in his anthology.

Several book-length examinations of the plays observe them as manifestations of language, a subject in which Shaw expressed profound interest all his life and which was, Shaw insisted, the basis of his most popular high comedy. (A collection of his relevant pronouncements, *Bernard Shaw on Language* [1963], is edited by Abraham Tauber.) *Shaw: The Style and the Man* (1962), by Richard Ohmann, is a lively and thorough analysis of Shaw's characteristic linguistic modes in his nondramatic prose, especially the prefaces to the plays. John A. Mills, in *Language and Laughter* (1969), extends linguistic analysis to the plays themselves and is particularly useful in examining Shaw's employment of dialect, automatism and wordplay, and linguistic satire. Fred Mayne, in *The Wit and Satire of Bernard Shaw* (1967), limits his study to the methods and subtleties of Shavian satire. Its isolation as a functional element has the drawback of disembodying Shaw's intellect from the rest of the playwright. The most searching linguistic analysis of Shaw appears as the lengthiest chapter in *Six Dramatists in Search of a Language* (1975), where Andrew Kennedy sees Shaw's attempts at linguistic naturalism "deflected by his emphatically different use of language," and concluding in the later plays—as a reflection of the breakdown of values—with a language that is only the thin edge between hope and despair. An entry with a different stylistic slant is David J. Gordon's *Bernard Shaw and the Comic Sublime* (1990), which posits "an accession of energy . . . in Shaw's language and theatre" through a hyperbolic, near-poetic "clarification of motive" or "an initiating act of transformative repudiation."

Criticism of the Shavian canon in individual chapters of more general books, or as articles or reviews, will largely be treated separately below under specific play titles; however, a dozen or more authors should be singled out for their range of coverage. Although Max Beerbohm retired as dramatic critic of the *Saturday Review* in 1910, he had reviewed every Shaw production in London since 1898, as well as the published novels and texts of plays not yet produced, and emerged from hostility and skepticism into grudging admiration for the theatrical qualities of Shaw's work. The selected reviews, published as *Around Theatres* in 1924, were supplemented posthumously into a complete run of the *Saturday Review* contributions via *More Theatres* (1969) and *Last Theatres* (1970) and have the added value of enabling one to view Shavian drama in the context of Edwardian theater. An even greater range is visible in Desmond MacCarthy's collected reviews in *Shaw* (1951), for MacCarthy was active as a theater critic for nearly half a century.

American critical journalism emerged nearly as early, in the work of H. L. Mencken and then of his colleague George Jean Nathan; however, the best American criticism in Shaw's lifetime came from Edmund Wilson, who began reviewing Shaw in *The New Republic* just after World War I and produced his most thoughtful analysis in "Bernard Shaw at Eighty" in *The Triple Thinkers* (1938), where he saw the principal pattern in Shaw ("aside from the duel between male and female") as "the polar opposition between the type of the saint and the type of the successful practical man." Writing for *The Nation* at the same time was Joseph Wood Krutch, who saw Shaw's dilemmas as those of the playwright who must fight his audience, rather than accept its prejudices, and then attempt to transcend in his later dramas (and in revivals of earlier ones) the paradox of his ideas and techniques having successfully become "the general background of twentieth-century thought" rather than remaining "the esoteric possession of a few." As drama critic and play-reader for the Theatre Guild, John Gassner covered the same span of years, his views on Shaw culminating in "Saint George and the Dragons" (in *The Theatre in Our Times,* 1954), in which he saw Shaw's achievement as reconciling the roles of preacher and dramatist—that it was often in his preachment that he found his art. Shaw, Gassner declared in many contexts over the years, "enriched the realistic substance of the drama by bringing economics and sociological realities into the theatre, and by turning the British drawing room into a forum, actually liberated the stage from the limitations of realism. He recalled the theatre to its classic and Elizabethan heritage of freedom from picayune illusionism; in other words, he drew close to the freedom of presentational as against representational art" ("Bernard Shaw and the Making of the Modern Mind," rpt. in *Dramatic Soundings,* 1968).

The most provocative criticism on Shaw's side of the Atlantic at the same time was Marxist. "Christopher Caudwell" (Christopher St. John Sprigg) published an invective-filled chapter on Shaw in his *Studies in a Dying Culture* (1936) in which G.B.S. is identified as the victim of "bourgeois illusions" despite his claims of identity with socialism. "From this . . . springs the unreality of his plays, their lack of dramatic resolutions, the substitute of debate for dialectic, the belief in life forces and thought Utopias, the bungling treatment of human beings in love, the lack of scientific knowledge and the queer strain of mountebank in all Shaw says." Erich Strauss, in *Bernard Shaw: Art and Socialism* (1942), with slightly more sympathy, examined the relationship between Shaw's plays and his politics and found them wanting as ideology although—for that very reason—successful as drama. Marxist in the Caudwell manner was Alick West, in *Bernard Shaw: A Good Man Fallen among Fabians* (1949—the title from a remark by Lenin, which Caudwell had quoted), who saw

Shaw's greatest weakness as "his isolation from the force that will make the future, the working-class movement of socialism." Yet he also saw Shaw as the first playwright to "break through the barrier, which most playwrights were too awed even to approach, . . . [of] the imaginary world of the drama against the forces of change in the world of reality; he had to create the means to express dramatically that the men and women on the stage were members of a society based on exploitation. He created these means."

In Shaw's last decade, overviews of his work came more and more to resolve, or at least blur, the complexities in his life and work. W. H. Auden in "The Fabian Figaro" (*Commonweal,* 1942) noted in referring to "the famous Shavian humor" that "at the bottom of everything comic lies a contradiction," one of these contradictions—despite Marxist objections—being that Shaw was "the only writer who had read Karl Marx with real profit." In the last analysis, however, he saw Shaw in musical terms—not as the Mozart of English drama described earlier by Edmund Wilson but as "the Rossini. . . . He has all the brio, the humor, the tunes, the clarity, and the virtuosity of that great master of Opéra Bouffé." Jacques Barzun's "Bernard Shaw in Twilight" (*KR,* 1943) saw Shaw at 87 as no longer having "a living reputation" but rather the legendary one of the classical artist, with Shaw's criticism likely to endure long after the works criticized were forgotten and the "salt of satire," the "great preservative," likely to keep his plays on the stage. To L. Kronenberger, publishing his dramatic lectures just after Shaw's death (*The Thread of Laughter,* 1952), balance was needed in any immediately posthumous appraisal, and he arrived at it by reminding readers of Shaw's "repetition, unevenness, self-indulgence, frivolity, exhibitionism," before he cited the brilliant vigor that Shaw brought to the dramatization of people and ideas. "What should be said at least is simply that here is one of the great masters of dialogue, one of the ablest writers of prose, in the whole range of English writing, whether drama or literature."

Although overviews continued to be written, even after the

inevitable spate of obituary notices in 1950–51 and centenary summations in 1956–57, the most useful writing about Shaw since this period lies in criticism of, and researches into, the individual plays and in approaches to the canon from special perspectives. Thus Donald Costello's *The Serpent's Eye: Bernard Shaw and the Cinema* (1965), precursor to Dukore's authoritative *Collected Screenplays,* ranges from *How He Lied to Her Husband* to the screen triumphs of *Pygmalion* and *Major Barbara,* the failures of the on-site spectacle *Caesar and Cleopatra,* and the posthumous *Androcles and the Lion.*

In *Bernard Shaw, Director* (1971), B. F. Dukore examines Shaw's vigorous direction of his own plays and his contribution toward modern directorial style. Earlier, in W. A. Armstrong's "George Bernard Shaw: The Playwright as Producer" (*MD,* 1966) and in S. P. Albert's "Shaw's Advice to the Players of *Major Barbara*" and "More Shaw Advice to the Players of *Major Barbara*" (*ThS,* 1969, 1970), a start had been made toward such analysis; while in "The Avant Garde Shaw," *Shaw,* [Festival] *Seminar Papers* (1965 and subsequent anthologized reprintings), S. Weintraub examines how Shaw's playwriting foreshadows developments later considered (in other playwrights from Brecht to Beckett) avant-garde and even "absurd." A number of critics have since developed this concept further. In "Discovering Shaw by Directing Shaw," *SHAW* 12 (1992), an effective director of Shaw, Stephen Porter, offers insights into the plays from a performance point of view, an angle taken up by a number of scholars in *SHAW* 3, *Shaw's Plays in Performance* (ed. D. J. Leary, 1983). Perhaps the most cogent short essay on the continuing liveliness of Shavian drama is M. Holroyd's "Shaw's Plays Go On Talking to Modern Audiences" in the *New York Times* (18 January 1987). Imaginative perspectives toward the plays are likely to enable us to view the canon from fresh yet valid angles and enlarge our vision of Shavian drama.

7

The Novels and Other Fiction

Although all five of Shaw's completed novels have been published—the first, *Immaturity* (written 1879) only in the collected editions—not all of them have been reprinted since. *Cashel Byron* emerged (ed. S. Weintraub, 1968) in a text that reproduces the first (1886) Modern Press edition with an appendix of variants from the *To-Day* serial text. The fragment of Shaw's sixth novel (written 1887–88) was published as *An Unfinished Novel by Bernard Shaw* (1958), edited and with a biographical introduction by S. Weintraub that identifies as a crucial source of inspiration the growing infatuation of Edith Bland ("E. Nesbit") for Shaw, later validated by the G.B.S. *Diaries.* Manuscripts of the novels, except for *Love among the Artists,* inadvertently carted off by the dustman except for scattered pages retrieved by the British bookseller Dan J. Rider, were presented by Shaw to the National Library of Ireland in 1946 (D. Rider, *Adventures with Bernard Shaw,* 1929).

Studies of the novels, individually and collectively, have faced from the start the competition of "Bernard Shaw's Works of

Fiction: Reviewed by Himself," *The Novel Review* (February 1892), which brilliantly analyzed the four published novels. An early bibliography is Maurice Holmes's *Some Bibliographical Notes on the Novels of George Bernard Shaw* (1928), and a detailed pamphlet on *An Unsocial Socialist* itself is F. E. Loewenstein's *The History of a Famous Novel* (1946). The best of the studies of the novels published in Shaw's lifetime is Claude Bissell's (*UTQ,* 1947), while the only books on the novels are R. F. Dietrich's *Portrait of the Artist as a Young Superman* (1969), which examines the fiction as the maturing of the Shavian personality, in the process emphasizing the first novel, *Immaturity*; and E. Nageswara Rao's slighter *Shaw the Novelist* (1959), more of a survey, which includes a chapter on the short fiction identified to that date, including at least one the *Diaries* prove to be instead a real-life vignette, "A Sunday on the Surrey Hills." The two most substantial studies, both of monograph length and both exploring the novels as foreshadowing the plays in plot, theme, and even in structure, are S. Weintraub, "The Embryo Playwright in Bernard Shaw's Early Novels" (*TSLL,* 1959) and Robert Hogan, "The Novels of Bernard Shaw" (*ELT,* 1965).

Useful articles on individual novels remain scarce. S. Weintraub's "Bernard Shaw, Charles Lever, and *Immaturity*" (*ShawR,* 1957) examines the novel's striking indebtedness, beyond its strong autobiographical element, to the Irish novelist's *A Day's Ride: A Life's Romance* (1863), which Shaw recalled reading as a boy. N. Grene's "The Maturity of *Immaturity*: Shaw's First Novel" (*IUR,* 1990) compares the text Shaw unsuccessfully hawked to publishers during 1879–81 to the revised 1923 text published later in the Collected Edition (some substantive alterations; two mice-nibbled chapters omitted). John Rodenbeck's "*The Irrational Knot* and the Uses of Ibsen" (*ShawR,* 1969) compares the serial and book texts, one written before Shaw knew Ibsen's work, the other after; and C. A. Berst's "*The Irrational Knot*: The Art of a Young Ibsenite" (*JEGP,* 1986), looking at the Ibsen foreshadowings, concludes that "moral originality" is a closer connection to the Norwegian than the *Doll's House* slamming of the door (by the husband in Shaw) at the close. Phyllis Goodman in "Beethoven as the Prototype of Owen Jack" (in *Love among the Artists*) uses Shaw's confession as her springboard and examines the biography of Beethoven to which the novel's Welsh protagonists owes much of his appearance and character. The only separate study of the ebullient *Cashel Byron's Profession* is S. Weintraub's introduction to his edition of the 1885–86 serial text in *To-Day* magazine (1968). Here the work is described as Shaw's parody of "a collection of absurd Victorian novelistic conventions while going his own fictional way." Two examinations of *An Unsocial Socialist,* the last completed novel, are S. Weintraub's "Genesis of a Play: Two Early Approaches to *Man and Superman*" (see the discussion of short fiction below), and Ryan Kiernan's "Citizens of Centuries to Come: The Ruling-class Rebel in Socialist Fiction," in *The Rise of Socialist Fiction* (ed. H. Gustav Klaus, 1987), in which Shaw's hero, Sidney Trefusis, is compared to Grant Allen's Ernest Le Breton of *Philistia* (1884), written a year later. The long introduction by S. Weintraub to *An Unfinished Novel* (see above under Editions) remains the only substantial study of the fictional fragment.

Not a Shaw work, but based on one, is Robert Hogan's dramatic adaptation of Shaw's novel *An Unsocial Socialist* (1978), which largely uses Shaw's dialogue and retains Shaw's title. (Another dramatic version of a Shaw novel was the English ITV production of *Love among the Artists*, 7 August 1979.)

The Adventures of the Black Girl in Her Search for God (1932), product of Shaw's South African adventure in Knysna, has appeared in several texts and under several modified titles. In 1934 Shaw altered the text to change "minus x" to "minus one," and "Myna's sex" to "Myna's one." Originally he had summed up the mystery of existence in the equation, "the square root of minus x." From the equation he created the Black Girl's innocent misconstruing of the concept with the sex of the goddess Myna. When charged with scientific inaccuracy, Shaw weakened the pun. Current editions restore it.

One such text, in *The Portable Bernard Shaw,* is prefaced by a letter, 30 January 1928, to the missionary Mabel Shaw, clearly the germ of the novella. Further background is detailed in Sean Morrow's "The Missionary in *The Black Girl*" (*SHAW* 6, 1986), about Mabel Shaw, her Girls' Boarding School in Northern Rhodesia (now Zambia), and her relationship with Shaw, who invited her to lunch in May 1930 when she was on home leave.

The most authoritative scholarship on *The Black Girl*, by L. H. Hugo, consists of two articles: "Upset in a Sun-Trap: Shaw in South Africa" (*SHAW* 5, 1985) and "The Black Girl and Some Lesser Quests: 1932–1934" (*SHAW* 9, 1989), which examines the rash of anti-G.B.S.—and some pro-G.B.S.—parodies of and polemics against *The Black Girl.*

Very little has appeared in print on Shaw's short fiction other than *The Black Girl,* although he had attempted short stories since his early twenties and had published several of them in the 1880s and even into the first decades of the new century. A minor addition to the canon is J. E. Bringle's first printing, with notes, of Shaw's 1879 prose sketch "The St James's Hall Mystery" (*BRH,* 1979), a rejected musical satire. Unidentified as Shaw's for nearly a century is "A.D: 3,000. The True Report of a County Councillor's Dream," a short story combining political prophecy and science fiction published first in *The Star,* London, 17 January 1889 and reprinted as Shaw's on the evidence of his diaries in *SHAW* 6 (1986). Long known as Shaw's but not reprinted or annotated until a century after are his contributions to a novel by several hands, *The Salt of the Earth* (*The World* [19 November 1890]), edited by Fred D. Crawford in *SHAW* 9, *Shaw Offstage* (1989).

The major—almost the only—study of Shaw's short fiction is by M. J. Holland in *SHAW* 9 (1989). "Shaw's Short Fiction: A Path to Drama" does not include, as does E. N. Rao's 1959 book, prose vignettes that are only faintly embellished autobiography, but Holland does identify stories both known and unknown to the *Bibliography* from the first printed fiction, "The Miraculous Revenge" (written 1881), to "The Emperor and the Little Girl" (published 1916), which S. Weintraub suggests in *Journey to*

Heartbreak tries out one of the concepts upon which the *Saint Joan* Epilogue is based. Examinations of individual short stories and fictionalizations include S. Weintraub's analysis of the origins and implications of the World War I fiction, "The Emperor and the Little Girl," in *Journey to Heartbreak* (1971); J. E. Bringle's previously mentioned "The St James's Hall Mystery," *BRH* 3 (1978), which prints an abortive story involving the ghost of Mozart; and R. Weintraub's " 'Mental Telegraphy?': Mark Twain on G.B.S." (*ShawR,* 1974), about Shaw's "Aerial Football" and a Mark Twain parallel. Although Shaw professed in his diary to be "greatly pleased" with a story he intended in 1887 for *Unwin's Annual,* "Don Giovanni Explains," it smelled too much of scandal for magazine publishers of his day and indeed was a thinly disguised retelling of his "seduction" by Mrs. Jane Patterson in July 1885. It was not published until the Collected Edition of 1932. An early examination of it as a foreshadowing of elements of *Don Juan in Hell* (1901–2) is S. Weintraub's "Genesis of a Play: Two Early Approaches to *Man and Superman,*" in *Shaw: Seven Critical Essays* (ed. N. Rosenblood, 1971).

8

Early Musical, Dramatic, and Literary Journalism

Dan H. Laurence's introductions to *How to Become a Musical Critic* (1961) and *Shaw's Music* (1981) are the most thorough analyses of Shaw as music reviewer. Biographically, the best sources remain Shaw himself and Rosset's *Shaw of Dublin* (for the Lee relationship). While George S. Barber (*PMLA,* 1957) offers a handy overview of the music criticism, it is dated by subsequent additions to the canon. Charles Rosen's "The Real Business of the Critic" (*TLC,* 25 December 1981) is more than a learned and lucid review of all of Shaw's music criticism; it has the added insights of a musicologist who is also an accomplished professional musician. While much has been written on Shaw's debt to music in his playwriting (see especially Coskren, Charles Loyd Holt, and Paulina Salz Pollak), and much more on the music criticism itself, little on the criticism is more than historical or biographical. Two of the more useful essays appear in *SHAW* 12 (1992), Richard Corballis's "Why the Devil Gets All the Good Tunes" and Josephine Lee's "The Skilled Voluptuary: Shaw as Music Critic."

The art criticism is less known. As "G.B.S." in *The World*, Shaw in the late 1880s inveighed against academic painting and praised the later Pre-Raphaelites and the Impressionists, while earlier he had championed the same causes in "Art Corner" columns in Annie Besant's socialist monthly *Our Corner*. Reprintings earlier than S. Weintraub's complete *Bernard Shaw on the London Art Scene 1885–1950* are four *World* reviews reprinted by Jack Kalmar in "Shaw on Art" (*MD*, 1959) and two 1886 "Art Corner" reviews in *ShawR* (1972). Shaw's "exploitation" of his immersion in art to create scenes, situations, and characters in his plays is explored by S. Weintraub (*MD*, 1975), augmented in *The Unexpected Shaw* and further revised in *London Art Scene*.

While Shaw's writings on photography have been collected almost completely in the Jay-Moore edition (see above under Editions), S. Weintraub's review of the volume in *History of Photography: An International Quarterly* (1989) adds two unsigned paragraphs from *The World* omitted from the book. G. Weales in *Georgia Review* (1990) uses his review for a rare reconsideration of Shaw's writings on photography, while Melinda Boyd Parsons in "The 'Unmechanicalness' of Photography: Bernard Shaw's Activist Photographic Philosophy," *CLQ* (1989) returns to Shaw's novel *An Unsocial Socialist* (to an extract reprinted by Jay and Moore) to find social implications in Shaw's ideas on photography. *ShawR* (1980) in "Temple Scott on Bernard Shaw" publishes "The Terrible Truthfulness of Mr. Shaw," a hitherto unknown early essay on truth and art via the camera.

An 1887 lecture, "Fiction and Truth," appears in *Bernard Shaw's Nondramatic Literary Criticism* (ed. S. Weintraub, 1972), the introduction to which is one of the few extended evaluations of Shaw as literary critic. (It is augmented in *Unexpected Shaw*.) Shaw's best-known criticism, *The Quintessence of Ibsenism* (1891), has been scrutinized in a number of articles, notably Daniel C. Gerould's (*CL*, 1963), which takes to task other critics for accusing Shaw of misrepresenting Ibsen. Shaw analyzes the plays as exposures of sham ideals, in his preface even declaring that his intention is not to examine the dramatics or poetics of the plays,

Gerould writes, for Shaw was introducing Ibsen to a *reading* public at a time when there was "no valid dramatic tradition" in which to visualize the playwright. Another useful study is John Gassner's "Shaw on Ibsen and the Drama of Ideas," in *Ideas and the Drama* (1964), reprinted in *Dramatic Soundings.* Again the charge that Shaw created Ibsen in his own image is refuted; his "provocative definition of Ibsenism" is seen, rather, as an introduction to "that considerable portion of the modern drama that exemplifies modern social and moral thought." However, Alan P. Barr's persuasive "Diabolonian Pundit: G.B.S. as Critic" (*ShawR,* 1968) examines Shaw's use of his criticism in general to proselytize, *The Quintessence of Ibsentism* not excluded. The most sound textual criticism is in Wisenthal's preface to *Shaw and Ibsen,* previously cited. Perhaps the most simplistic is Keith May's *Ibsen and Shaw* (1985), which defines Ibsen as tragedian and Shaw as comedian because "Tragedy tends to ennoble the spectators, comedy to vulgarize them."

The "other" major critical essay, *The Perfect Wagnerite* (1896), has received less critical attention but is the subject of a thorough examination by William Blissett (*UTQ,* 1957–58), who concludes that as long as Shaw found a kindred intellectual and spiritual soul in Wagner he was contentedly Wagnerian but that Shaw deliberately ignored his hero's shift to conservatism and love worship. Janice Henson (*ShawR,* 1961) notes, however, that "It is curious that the very point at which Shaw boggles is the one most typical of Wagner's operas as a whole, and the one which his interpreters generally find easiest to accept, . . . the search for redemption through love." Informed by a mutual attraction to authoritarian leadership is Oswald Mosley's pamphlet *Wagner and Shaw: A Synthesis* (1956). A. Ganz's brief introductory study, *George Bernard Shaw,* is particularly insightful on Wagner-Shaw influences, subject of an earlier essay by him, "The Playwright as Perfect Wagnerite" (*CD,* 1979). Other significant essays on this aspect of Shaw are Wisenthal's "The Underside of Undershaft: A Wagnerian Motif in *Major Barbara*" (*ShawR,* 1972) and R. Coskren's "*Siegfried* Elements in Shaw's Plays" (*SHAW* 2, 1982).

Criticism and research have largely neglected the other polemical writings—the political, philosophical, social, and economic articles, treatises, and books. E. Strauss's *Bernard Shaw: Art and Socialism* (1942) remains the standard Marxist account of Shaw's social and economic writings, with no comparable examination from another perspective. S. Weintraub's *Journey to Heartbreak* analyzes the origins and impact of the myriad World War I writings, many but not all of them reprinted in the Collected Edition, vol. 21, *What I Really Wrote about the War*; and here it might be noted, too, that Gordon N. Bergquist's *The Pen and the Sword: War and Peace in the Prose and Plays of Bernard Shaw* (1977) attempts to pull together Shaw's ideas on war and peace, concluding that Shaw's philosophical positions tend predictably to be pragmatic rather than polemically consistent.

Dan H. Laurence and D. H. Greene have collected most of the writings about Ireland into *The Matter with Ireland* (1962), which annotates biographical and historical obscurities. Here it is worth observing that with few exceptions, Irish critics and commentators since Shaw's own day have deplored both his plays and his attitudes toward Irish issues of every kind, alleging or implying that Shaw distanced himself from the realities of Ireland.

Other Shavian economic and social writings have been noted in the collections of his essays and lectures above. These collections have provoked little criticism or evaluation.

9

Criticism of Individual Plays

The quantity and range of criticism of individual Shavian plays seem to be a reflection of the depths that critics feel can be sounded rather than an index to their popularity in performance, although in a few cases—*Candida*, *Pygmalion*, and *Man and Superman*, for example—critics and audiences seem equally bemused. More and more research and criticism are being directed toward the less produced plays, partly because the soil is less tilled but partly, too, because their political, philosophical, and technical complexities were in advance of their time and can now be better understood.

Passion Play

Shaw's first serious play attempt, an unfinished blank verse biblical parable begun in 1878, was first published in 1971 as

Passion Play (ed. J. E. Bringle). Beyond the editor's brief prefatory account of its composition and abandonment in the second act, there is an analysis of its autobiographical content in R. Weintraub's "Shaw's Jesus and Judas" (*ShawR*, 1972) and additional biographical probing in I. Lindblad's " 'Household of Joseph': An Early Perspective on Shaw's Dramaturgy" (*ShawR*, 1974). C. A. Berst's "In the Beginning: The Poetic Genesis of Shaw's God" (*SHAW* 1, 1981) finds a "lively dialectic, a poetically charged ambiguity," in the clash between Judas and Jesus. In his *Bishop of Everywhere*, W. S. Smith reminds us that the forty-nine-page holograph fragment (BL) is actually titled by Shaw *The Household of Joseph* and begins "promisingly" with a cast of characters headed by "Jesus, illegitimate son of Mary." The verse, like the theology, Smith observes, is "more Shelleyan than Shakespearean."

Widowers' Houses

Shaw's first completed play, *Widowers' Houses* (produced 1892), has been the subject of little useful research and criticism other than in book-length studies, although Charles Shattuck's "Bernard Shaw's 'Bad Quarto' " (*JEGP*, 1955), which studies the 1893 and 1898 printed text versions of *Widowers' Houses*, remains a model of its kind, and in it Shaw's developing professionalism as a playwright is palpable. (Few similar studies of Shavian printed texts exist, among them H. M. Geduld's on *Back to Methuselah* [*ShawR*, 1962] and B. F. Dukore's "Toward an Interpretation of *Major Barbara*" [*ShawR*, 1963]. The best critical analysis of Shaw's dramatic strategy in *Widowers' Houses* remains C. A. Carpenter's in his *Art of Destroying Ideals*. Worth notice are two articles (both in *ShawR*, 1975)—Kinley E. Roby's "Stap Street to Robbins' Row," which discusses the relationship of the play to the Report of the Royal Commission on the Housing of the

Working Classes, and Diderik Roll-Hansen's "Sartorius and the Scribes of the Bible: Satiric Method in *Widowers' Houses*," which sees the biblical association in the title as less farfetched than Shaw contended.

An illuminating book could be compiled from the reactions, pro and con, of Shaw's noncritic contemporaries to his plays, beginning with the very first of them. While the newspaper press was apoplectic, and even such drama-reviewer friends of his as William Archer were both publicly and privately scornful, E. M. Forster would recall in "Notes on the Way," in *Time and Tide* (1934), "Ever since I have read *Widowers' Houses* I have felt hopeless about investments. It seemed impossible for a small private investor like myself to know where his money had actually gone or whether it was doing harm or good. . . . I have got to feel that the world of finance is so complicated that—ethically speaking—it doesn't matter what I buy. In a sense this is true. It is impossible for any one to have clean hands. . . . No individual, however humble, can be guiltless."

The Philanderer

The Philanderer, Shaw's second completed play, has provoked little research and less useful criticism, B. F. Tyson being responsible for the only studies of its development. "Shaw's First Discussion Play: An Abandoned Act of *The Philanderer*" (*ShawR*, 1969) describes an abandoned eighty-eight-page draft of a discursive act on the marriage question and the problem of divorce, questions later taken up in the discussion play *Getting Married*. "One Man and His Dog: A Study of a Deleted Draft of Bernard Shaw's *The Philanderer*" (*MD*, 1967) describes an abandoned "Gilbertian plot." Shaw had difficulties developing a play in which his ideas would cohere, a point later made by Novick in his Garland "Early Texts" preface. Carpenter (in *Ideals*) examines the play's undermining of "the capitalist institution of marriage," and Morgan (in *Playground*) contends that "the true tension and conflict in the play . . . arise from the author's recognition that there is a negative and potentially dangerous side to the exercise of reason and its control of emotion." Turco, in "*The Philanderer*: Shaw's Poignant Romp" in *SHAW* 7, *The Neglected Plays* (1987), for which he is guest editor, reviews the work "as submerged autobiography, refurbished Restoration comedy, and topical satire," and goes beyond to see the play as "most Ibsenian precisely in its satire of programmatic Ibsenism."

Mrs Warren's Profession

Shaw's third play has attracted commentators from the start. Tyson, in "Shaw among the Actors: Theatrical Additions to *Plays Unpleasant*" (*MD*, 1971), has examined revisions Shaw made in all three "unpleasant plays" prior to publication in 1898, particularly in sharpening stage directions. Another an enlightening study of Shaw's development as a dramatist as he wrote *Mrs Warren's Profession* in 1893 is B. G. Knepper's "Shaw Rewriting Shaw: A Fragment" (*ShawR*, 1969), which compares versions of the third (and last) act, finding "little more than unrelieved melodramatic mawkishness" in the first version, while "the second moves toward genuine dramatic force," and the third "achieves it." Shaw's development of the well-made play inherited from French masters and English imitators into a dramatic form uniquely his own is described in Stephen Stanton's "Shaw's Debt to Scribe" (*PMLA*, 1961) and in Eric Bentley's standard "The Making of a Dramatist (1892–1903)" (*TDR*, 1960). Bentley's analysis of Shavian structure and the "emotional substance" that fleshes it out demonstrates how Shaw's use of reversal and anticlimax transforms the Scribean method and creates thinking audiences by upsetting their expectations. Tracy Simmons

Bitonti's "Shaw's Offstage Characters" (*SHAW* 12, 1992), while of general interest, is of special utility here because so many offstage figures in *Mrs Warren's Profession* influence the action. (Other plays for which Bitonti's essay is helpful are *Man and Superman*, *Candida*, *John Bull's Other Island*, *Getting Married*, *Major Barbara*, *Heartbreak House*, and *The Apple Cart*.)

The literary background of the play in French fiction is established by Geoffrey Bullough in "Literary Relations of Shaw's Mrs Warren" (*PQ*, 1962), which also analyzes sources from life. Bullough discusses Guy de Maupassant's *Yvette*, Janet Achurch's *Mrs. Daintree's Daughter* (borrowed from *Yvette*), and the real-life Arabella Susan Lawrence (a mathematics student from Newnham College, Cambridge, and a suffragist and socialist), whom Shaw knew from London political life. From the literary standpoint a major omission is repaired in Betty Freeman Johnson's "Shelley's *Cenci* and *Mrs Warren's Profession*" (*ShawR*, 1972), which validates Shaw's declaration to Archer in an 1893 letter that he had "skillfully blended the plot of the Second Mrs Tanqueray with that of the Cenci." Stephen R. Grecco adds several suggestions from life in Shaw's own strong-minded and independent mother and sister in "Vivie Warren's Profession" (*ShawR*, 1967), suggesting, too, lesbian tendencies in Vivie Warren—an allegation opposed by Marlie P. Wasserman (*ShawR*, 1972). V. Rao's "Vivie Warren in the Blakean World of Experience" (*ShawR*, 1979) links *Mrs Warren's Profession* to Blake's early ideas of innocence and experience. (Shaw in the 1890s professed great indebtedness to Blake.) In "Vivie Warren and the Tripos" (*ShawR*, 1980), William A. Dolid reconstructs what Vivie Warren's academic triumph at Newnham involved and puts the achievement in the context of a woman's place at Cambridge in Vivie's supposed time. In Berst's "Propaganda and Art in *Mrs Warren's Profession*" (*Art of Drama*), the drama is seen as a morality play, with Vivie tempted, but spurning the bait for freedom; contemporary morality is examined with respect to the first U.S. production in 1905 (and the verdict is harsh) by George E. Wellwarth (*ShawR*, 1959).

Arms and the Man

Arms and the Man, completed and produced in 1894, has been performed far more than it has been examined. The standard study of its sources is L. Crompton's chapter on the play in *Shaw the Dramatist*, where the play is described as having thrown overboard "the whole of Victorian moral rhetoric . . . for a utilitarian, naturalistic ethic." C. A. Berst's "Romance and Reality in *Arms and the Man*" (*MLQ*, 1966), like his other essays adapted into his *Bernard Shaw and the Art of Drama*, suggests penetratingly that the comedy "expresses the interlocking relationship and mutual dependence of romanticism and realism." As in so many other instances, the most probing look at a Shaw play is Shaw's own, in this case his partly tongue-in-cheek "A Dramatic Realist to His Critics" (*New Review*, July 1894), several times reprinted and crucial to all critics, and his 1894 letters to William Archer (in *CL*). In "Shaw's Use of Vergil's *Aeneid* in *Arms and the Man*" (*ShawR*, 1976), Calvin T. Higgs, Jr., suggests not only that the paradoxical title is adapted from Vergil but that the play demonstrates an intimate knowledge of the epic and follows the structural and thematic construction of the Dido episode. Samuel Weiss examines Shaw's use of Bulgarian war facts in an essay in *SHAW* 10 (1990).

Candida

Candida, also completed in 1894, mesmerized researchers and critics from the start. A useful collection of criticism is S. Stanton's *A Casebook on Candida* (1962), which brings together commentary by Shaw and others and extracts portions of texts influential in the intellectual background of the play from De Quincey to Carlyle and Nietzsche. (Stanton's "Debt to Scribe" article is also predominantly an analysis of *Candida*.) Other studies of the play's intellectual background, with emphasis on character prototypes, includes Nethercot's "Who *Was* Eugene Marchbanks?" (*ShawR*, 1972), which sums up the cases for various prototypes from life and awards the palm to Shelley on the basis of echoes and analogues in the play; and Crompton's *Shaw* chapter on *Candida*, which makes a case for the effete young Yeats Shaw knew in the early 1890s, as does S. Weintraub's "Uneasy Friendship: Shaw and Yeats" (*Yeats*, 1983), where the poet's work and personality are seen in Marchbanks. Barbara Peart's "De Quincey and Marchbanks" (*ShawR*, 1974) sustains Shaw's contention that Marchbanks is based upon the young De Quincey via analogues with the David Masson 1887 biography of De Quincey owned by Henry Salt and very likely read by Shaw. (Shaw's *Diaries 1885–1897* now prove that he read Masson.)

"Pre-Raphaelite Drama: *Candida*," in E. B. Adams's *Shaw and the Aesthetes* sees the play as a "Shavian mystery play about Madonna and Child"—a viewpoint Shaw gave cause to accept in a famous letter to Ellen Terry—and also as about the Pre-Raphaelite idealizing of woman and of artistic purpose. A parallel perspective is Gail Finney's "The New Woman as Madonna: Shaw's Candida," in her *Women in Modern Drama: Freud, Feminism and European Theatre at the Turn of the Century* (1990), where Candida is "That engaging amalgam of Virgin Mary and New Woman."

The standard critique of *Candida* remains E. Bentley's, elaborated in many places but first set forth in detail in *The Playwright as Thinker* (1946), which sees the play in its ambiguities as more than the "life-illusion of Ibsenic proportions" of Candida's husband Morell. Nethercot's provocative thesis ("The Truth about *Candida*," *PMLA*, 1949) that the three major characters represent Shaw's dramatizing of the three basic character types he formulated in *The Quintessence of Ibsenism* (Realist, Idealist, and Philistine) offers insight into Shaw's early dramaturgy that appears useful if not applied too rigidly. Berst (in *Art*) provides a persuasive defense of the naive Morell and concludes that his "smug" wife Candida "is not quite worth the fuss." And he escapes the inhibitions of previous critics by elaborating on the sexual imagery in the opening tableau and subsequent confrontation scene in act 3. "Such extensive and pointed sexual innuendo is unique in Shaw," according to Berst. "One would like to speculate that Shaw, still burning over the censor's rejection of *Mrs Warren's Profession*, is, incidentally, mocking that man's obtuseness, sailing by him with a smile." The sexual double entendres seem unquestionable; however, their inspiration may have appeared obvious to Janet Achurch, the Ibsenist actress for whom Shaw created the role of Candida and in whose marital life Shaw played a more persuasive Marchbanks.

Unique among critiques in Charles Loyd Holt's "*Candida*: The Music of Ideas," *ShawR* (1966), which sees the dialogue in musical terms, contending "that controlled repetition of language, idea or symbol is basic to surrogate 'musical' structure in drama." And he sees "motif balance, implied action or characterization, and the actual music patterns of phrase-groups, sectional song forms, the rondo, the sonata-allegro, the complete sonata, the fugue, and the several contrapuntal devices of imitation, canon, inversion, augmentation, diminutation. . . ."

The Man of Destiny

The Man of Destiny, Shaw's short play about the young Napoleon written in 1895 for Henry Irving (who never played it), has elicited little research and less useful criticism. The standard account of its backgrounds may be Martin Meisel's analysis of its strain of Scribe-Sardou romance, in which Shaw—in effect—remakes Sardou's *Madame Sans-Gêne*, a play he reviewed the year he wrote his own, observing in the process that Napoleon was "inscrutable, . . . as becomes a Man of Destiny" (*Shaw and the Nineteenth Century Theater*). R. N. Roy's chapter in *George Bernard Shaw's Historical Plays* (1976) attempts to document the authenticity of Shaw's portrait of Napoleon, as does Norbert Greiner in "Idealism *und* Realism *im Früwerk George Bernard Shaws*," in *Die Bedeutung und Funktion der Begriffe in den politischen, äesthetischen und dramatischen Schriften* (1977), and, also, J. Keunen in "*Napoleon in Shaviaanse stijl*," *Dietsche Warande en Belfort* (1970). Going beyond history to see the play as a "fusion" of "melodrama and antitheater" is Berst's "*The Man of Destiny*: Shaw, Napoleon, and the Theatre of Life," in *SHAW* 7 (1987).

The Devil's Disciple

The Devil's Disciple, another product of Shaw's then-active penchant for rewriting history, has been produced far more often but apparently has been considered almost equally lacking in such subtleties as attract critics. His confessed indebtedness to Blake (in his remarks prefacing the play) is briefly examined by Irving Fiske (*Shavian*, 1951; rpt. in R. J. Kaufmann, *G. B. Shaw: A Collection of Critical Essays*, 1965), who says little about the Blakean element in *The Devil's Disciple*. Two useful background studies of the play are Walter L. Royall's (*ShawR*, 1967) on Shaw's reliance on E. B. DeFonblanque's 1876 biography for his acerbic yet admiring portrait of General Burgoyne, and Raymond S. Nelson's (*ELT*, 1969), comparing the devil-hero of Robert Buchanan's narrative poem "The Devil's Case: A Bank-Holiday Interlude" (1896) with Dick Dudgeon, who, however derivative—Shaw had read the verses—is rather an agent of vitalism. Meisel's book covers nineteenth-century melodramas Shaw knew in which attractive scapegraces get in and out of familiar predicaments, from Dion Boucicault's stage success *Arrah-na-Pogue* (1864) to Charles Dickens's novel *A Tale of Two Cities* (dramatized in 1860), the ending of which Shaw quickly confessed he had satirized. Shaw himself provided background on the development of the play in "Trials of a Military Dramatist," *Review of the Week*

(4 November 1899), while the most useful general critical study in book form—and one of the rare extended studies of the play—is a chapter in Crompton's *Shaw*, which includes material from play manuscripts. S. Weintraub's "Exploiting Art" chapter of *The Unexpected Shaw* includes the *Tale of Two Cities* illustration by Frederick Barnard, *Sydney Carton* (at the scaffold), which Shaw declared was his inspiration for the concluding scene.

Two other studies lift the play from Shaw's own description of it as "threadbare melodrama." R. F. Whitman's "The Passion of Dick Dudgeon" (*ShawR*, 1978) elucidates the work as a passion play, with Dick "acting out the central Christian myth, and suffering a kind of passion in his betrayal, trial, and near-execution." (For the play as doppelgänger self-discovery, see below under *The Doctor's Dilemma* and J. Bertolini.) R. Weintraub's " 'Only the man . . . draws clear of it': A New Look at Anthony Anderson" (*ShawR*, 1980) perceives the common misunderstanding of Shaw's remark to Ellen Terry, that in every play he had written to that point he had "Prostituted the actress more or less by making the interest in her partly a sexual interest: only the *man* in *The Devil's Disciple* draws clear of it." Paradoxically, the man may be Anthony Anderson, Judith's husband, rather than Dick Dudgeon, with whom she is smitten even though Dick claims no amatory interest. A feminist slant is Carol Riddle's "Mrs. Dudgeon: More Sinned Against than Sinning," in *SHAW* 12 (1992).

You Never Can Tell

You Never Can Tell (1896), Shaw's subversive venture into fashionable West End comedy, completed before his inversion of popular melodrama in *The Devil's Disciple*, has been unpopular with critics and scholars. Louis Coxe's *Enabling Acts: Selected Essays in Criticism* (1977) reprints his 1955 essay on the play in which

Coxe observes, "The masters of reality, the cosmic dentists, of Shaw's drama are forever begging us to have it out. . . . Valentine is the actual dentist; Bohun is the spiritual dentist." Representative of the rise in esteem for the play is F.P.W. McDowell's "Shaw's 'Higher Comedy' Par Excellence," *SHAW* 7 (1987), which examines it as illustrating "the quintessential universal movement of comic art as Northrop Frye formulates it, 'from a society controlled by habit, ritual bondage, arbitrary law and the older characters [in the drama] to a society controlled by youth and pragmatic freedom, . . . a movement from illusion to reality.' "

Linda Herr's "Dickens' Jaggers and Shaw's Bohun: A Study of 'Character-Lifting' " (*ShawR*, 1977) is self-evident. Another background study is S. Weintraub's "G.B.S. Borrows from Sarah Grand: *The Heavenly Twins* and *You Never Can Tell*" (*Unexpected Shaw*), which concludes that the forgotten but once scandalous Ibsenite novel, despite sentimental and obtrusive moralizing, "seems to have provided Shaw with some of what he needed to develop a comedy which went beyond the illusions of conventional love to show its biological and irrational truth, and went beyond the illusions of fast-fading Victorian parent-child relationships to show them unsentimentally and unsparingly."

A chapter in Margery Morgan's *The Shavian Playground*, "Making the Skeleton Dance," suggests commedia dell'arte origins (in particular seeing the comic twins, Philip and Dolly, as Harlequin and Columbine) as well as patterns of Dionysian ritual. Maurice Valency's analysis in *The Cart and Trumpet* observes that Shaw aimed at "a level of comedy in which farcical situations would be given something like tragic weight. In some sense this was the contrary of Ibsen's method. The improbabilities of *You Never Can Tell*, its extraordinary encounters and coincidences, are acceptable only on the level of farce; but they were intended to have the force of parable. The *reductio ad absurdum* of the norms of social behavior would then have a moral connotation, and the jest would imply a sermon." Gibbs concludes that "the materials of farce become the basis of high comedy," and that in Shaw's play is "a celebration . . . of life's contradictions of expectation, system and reason." In the same vein, J. P. Smith in "Bernard Shaw and the Melting Mood," *WascanaR* 9 (1974), sees farcical conventions transmuted into humane comedy. Once neglected onstage, it is now a staple of Shavian repertory.

Caesar and Cleopatra

The historical basis of Shaw's first major history lesson, *Caesar and Cleopatra*, has been researched with thoroughness. Gordon W. Couchman's "Here Was a Caesar: Shaw's Comedy Today" (*PMLA*, 1957) examines how and if the playwright used the classical source material he publicly credited (such as Plutarch and Suetonius); and Gale K. Larson (*ShawR*, 1971), using G.B.S. correspondence not available earlier to Couchman, traces the development of Shaw's search for and use of historical material. Couchman's expansion of his Caesar essay is *This Our Caesar: A Study of Caesar and Cleopatra* (1974). Larson's edition of *Caesar and Cleopatra* (1974) includes an introductory discussion of Shaw's sources and reprints a number of Shavian commentaries on the play, including a 1945 letter to the editor of *The Times* of London. One of Shaw's major sources for his *Caesar*, and his likely justification for Cleopatra's youth and Caesar's asexual relationship with her (both useful for his purposes but violations of fact), is Theodor Mommsen's *History of Rome* (English trans. 1862–66); Shaw's use of it is explored by S. Weintraub in "Shaw's Mommsenite Caesar" (*Anglo-German and American-German Crosscurrents* 2, ed. P. A. Shelley and A. O. Lewis, 1962; augmented in *Unexpected Shaw*), findings afterward confirmed by several pages of notes by Shaw on Mommsen dated 1898 and reproduced in Crompton's *Shaw* from University of Texas holdings. Another perspective on Shaw's use of history is Otto Reinert's "Old History and New: Anachronism in *Caesar and Cleopatra*" (*MD*, 1960), the author finding amid all the apparent anachronisms that it is progress that is a myth and that the only real anachronism is Caesar, who is a human being ahead of his time, the incipient *Übermensch*.

Two studies point to Shaw's use of pictorial materials in his research: George W. Whiting's "The Cleopatra Rug Scene: Another Source" (*ShawR*, 1960) and Martin Meisel's "Cleopatra and 'The Flight into Egypt' " (*ShawR*, 1964). In "Exasperated Admiration: Bernard Shaw on Queen Victoria" (*VP*, 1987), S. Weintraub looks at how the play's subtext becomes a gloss upon Victoria's relations with two of her prime ministers, Melbourne and Disraeli, as well as upon other aspects of the Queen's personality, particularly in her years as a near-child monarch, having ascended to the throne in 1837 as an especially innocent eighteen-year-old.

Critical studies of the play are numerous, particularly those involving Shakespeare and Shaw. Accepting the carefully question-marked bait G.B.S. offered in the title to one section of the preface to his *Three Plays for Puritans*, "Better than Shakespear?" Couchman has produced two significant critiques of the play, one on the Shakespeare-Shaw theme: "*Antony and Cleopatra* and the Subjective Convention" (*PMLA*, 1961) and "Comic Catharsis in *Caesar and Cleopatra*" (*ShawR*, 1960). C. A. Berst (*JEGP*, 1969) examines the artistic devices used to convey a sense of Caesar's greatness; H. Ludeke, in "Some Remarks on Shaw's History Plays" (*ES*, 1955), takes the view that Shaw's own need for a hero image made creative demands upon the portrait he received from history that were too great to resist. Perhaps the most penetrating analysis is by D. J. Leary (*ShawR*, 1962), who formulates a theory of "dialectic action" in Shavian drama. In this case the antithesis, "the commonsense sphere of practical consideration" (closed morality), collides with the thesis, "the poet-philosopher's longer view of life" (open morality), to produce as its synthesis an incarnation of "ideal values," here seen but fleetingly in the Life Force's occasional Supermen, but someday to be widespread in the "long-desired social millenium." Leary applies his post-Bergsonian "dialectical action" theory to other plays, including *Major Barbara* and *Heartbreak House*.

Caesar and Cleopatra is examined from the perspective of religion in J. L. Wisenthal's "Shaw and Ra: Religion and Some History Plays" and in C. A. Berst's "In the Beginning: The Poetic Genesis of Shaw's God" (both in *SHAW* 1, 1981) and from the standpoint of myth in Timothy Vesonder's "Shaw's Caesar and the Mythic Hero" (*ShawR*, 1978), which shows how Shaw shaped Caesar to make him both archetypal and acceptably realistic and down-to-earth.

Captain Brassbound's Conversion

Captain Brassbound's Conversion, Shaw's last nineteenth century play, has been examined little more often than it has been performed. G.B.S., punning upon Shelley's poem, once noted that a tentative title for the play had been "The Witch of Atlas." Roland Duerksen studies the suggestion seriously (*ShawR*, 1972), and finds Lady Cicely's success in making

> All harsh and crooked purposes more vain
> Than in the desert in the serpent's wake
> Which the sand covers . . .

one of the many parallels between Shelley's witch and Shaw's lady. (On Shelley and Shaw in general, see Duerksen, *PMLA*, [1963], and Shaw/Shelley issue of *ShawR*, 1972.) G.B.S. himself detailed his indebtedness to R. W. Cunninghame Graham's travel book *Mogreb-el-Acksa* in his *Plays for Puritans* preface, and his further indebtedness to the personality of his friend Graham (particularly for the character of Sergius in *Arms and the Man*) has also long been known. His relations with Graham and their impact on his plays are summed up by John Walker in "Bernard

Shaw and Don Roberto" (*ShawR*, 1972). Another debt is exposed in S. Weintraub's "Shaw's Lady Cicely and Mary Kingsley" in *Fabian Feminist*, rpt. in *The Unexpected Shaw* (with additions), where parallels are seen in the intrepid lady explorer's *Travels in West Africa* (1897). "No witch, Mary Kingsley nevertheless prevailed in her African travels as if she were one." Mac E. Barrick (*ShawR*, 1978) looks at Lady Cicely's delightful "cognatic translation of the legal maxim *Fiat justitia ruat coelum*": "Let justice be done though the ceiling fall!" Ina Rae Hark evaluates the play from a conversion perspective in "Lady Cicely, I Presume: Converting the Heathen, Shavian Style" (*SHAW* 1, 1981).

In her introduction to the Garland "Early Texts" edition of the play, R. Weintraub examines Shaw's recent marriage to the independent-minded Charlotte as an influence on the characterization of Lady Cicely Waynflete, and looks at Shaw as "the bridegroom who has actually taken on a commander in chief as his wife and who may, like Brassbound, wonder if she is 'made to be something better than the wife of Black Paquito.' "

Of the few extended studies of this comic melodrama two are particularly valuable—Bentley's in *The Playwright as Thinker*, analyzing its central ironies, and Maurice Valency's in *The Cart and Trumpet*, which sees the play as a surprisingly successful "mixture of styles," Shaw's "workmanship in fitting together these random elements . . . of the rough-and-ready sort appropriate to a type of drama not intended for close scrutiny."

Man and Superman

Man and Superman (written 1901–2) has inspired a critical bibliography of immense proportions, with Shaw's own prefaces to the play and to the later *Back to Methuselah* among the most useful glosses. No close textual analysis of the play exists, perhaps because Shaw has frightened off most textual critics through his own passion for accuracy in seeing his work through the press; however, James Redmond has noted in "A Misattributed Speech in *Man and Superman*" (*TLS*, 18 January 1974) that act 1 lines by Octavius run into a two-sentence speech that should be spoken by Ann Whitefield. The error persisted into the Bodley Head Shaw, as did a misprint in the preface (vol. 2, 494) misquoting the *mille e tre* (a thousand and three) in the *Don Giovanni* "catalogue aria" of Leporello as "*mille etre* adventures" (Robertson Davies, *TLS*, 15 February 1974). Such textual slips are rare in Shaw.

For Shaw's use of the Don Juan myth, persuasive evaluations of the evidence are Oscar Mandel's *The Theatre of Don Juan* (1963), R. J. Blanch's (*RLV*, 1967), and Carl Mills's (*CL*, 1967). These (as well as many other studies) describe Shaw's inversion of the archetypal virile lover and seducer into the prey of the female, but none refer to Shaw's own precursors of the plot and theme, as does S. Weintraub (in *Shaw: Seven Critical Essays*, ed. N. Rosenblood, 1971), who examines both Shaw's 1887 autobiographical short story "Don Giovanni Explains" and his 1883 novel *An Unsocial Socialist* as early working models for *Man and Superman*. C. L. Holt's "Mozart, Shaw and *Man and Superman*" (*ShawR*, 1966) is a reliable investigation into how Shaw used the opera *Don Giovanni*, including close approximations of actual lines from the libretto, to arrive at his "deliberate inversion, . . . shaping *Man and Superman* out of the world's memory of Don Giovanni." Joseph Bentley (*ShawR*, 1968) goes further by suggesting that even the collapse of Tanner's resistance in the last act is an echo out of his mythic past, an allusion to the last act of *Don Giovanni* where the statue gives the hero a final chance to repent before dragging him off to hell. Using persuasive line-by-line parallels between opera libretto and Shaw's play, P. S. Pollak in "Master to the Masters: Mozart's Influence on Bernard Shaw's *Don Juan in Hell*" (*SHAW* 8, 1988) shows how structural patterns as well as dialogue come in part from *Don Giovanni*.

Numerous studies examine the theoretical basis of Shaw's play, the fullest of these being two by Carl Henry Mills: "Shaw's Debt to Lester Ward in *Man and Superman*" (*ShawR*, 1971), where sociologist Ward's "gynaeocentric" theory on female selection and evolution is seen as central to Shaw's ideas on Creative Evolution; and "Shaw's Theory of Creative Evolution" (*ShawR*, 1973), which examines the evolution of Shaw's thinking on the subject in general. A source study by David H. Bowman, "The Eugenicist's Handbook" (*ShawR*, 1975), examines the impact of Francis Galton and Karl Pearson on Shaw's eugenic ideas.

Shaw himself observed (in the Preface to *Back to Methuselah*) that his ingenuity in *Man and Superman* may have been counter-productive. "The effect was so vertiginous, apparently, that nobody noticed the new religion in the center of the intellectual whirlpool." Louis Kronenberger in *The Thread of Laughter* (1952) refers to the Hell scene's "defects of logic, its perversities of temperament," and Berst (in *Art*) sees Shaw as compromising his argument through the very dramatic controls he exerts over his dialectic in the debate in Hell. "While the wit and drama render the cosmology vital, the philosophy seems more dramatic than sound, the beauty of the rhetorical pyrotechnics more satisfying than the logic of the discourse."

The standard critical study of *Man and Superman* remains F. P. W. McDowell's "Heaven, Hell and Turn-of-the-Century London: Reflections upon Shaw's *Man and Superman*" (*DramaS*, 1963), to which Crompton, Valency, Morgan, and others acknowledge indebtedness for its interpretations of the relationships between the frame play and the play-within-the-play. Much the same area is covered by J. L. Wisenthal (*Marriage of Contraries*). Shaw's ingenuity in what Jean-Claude Amalric labels "intertextuality" is analyzed in his "Shaw's *Man and Superman* and the Myth of Don Juan: Intertextuality and Irony," *CVE* (April 1991), where Don Juan and *Don Giovanni* allusions are shown as slyly foreshadowing the dream interlude in the frame play. (It might also be noted that dream allusions are tucked into the frame play, both before and after the "Don Juan in Hell" interlude.)

Sally Peters Vogt's essay in *Fabian Feminist* sees Ann Whitefield not only as Shaw's "prototype of predatory females" but as a mythic figure whose role of "Woman Incarnate . . . subsumes all other roles," and Everywoman in both play and frame play. D. J. Leary (*ShawR*, 1979) elucidates the play from a Freudian perspective but observes, too, that Shaw's emphasis on female sexuality went beyond Freud, and that Freud objected to Shaw's "differing conceptions of womanhood." A much different approach to the play is taken by Albert Bermel (*ShawR*, 1975), who writes that because of the humor, "critics have continually failed to appreciate that his wit reaches below the lines and situations and character quirks: it saturates the play's very grain. Underlying the jesting is the super jest. . . ."

Little has been done to examine Shaw's appendices to the play, "John Tanner's *The Revolutionist's Handbook and Pocket Companion* and *Maxims for Revolutionists*"; however, C. A. Carpenter, in "Notes on Some Obscurities in 'The Revolutionist's Handbook' " (*ShawR*, 1970), has made a start toward rendering the topical allusions in the *Handbook* intelligible to modern readers, while Richard Ohmann's *Shaw: The Style and the Man* analyzes the prose of the *Handbook* as well as Shaw's method of developing "Tanner's" argument.

John Bull's Other Island

John Bull's Other Island (1904) has been receiving more stage and scholarly attention in recent years, after decades of undeserved neglect. W. S. Smith (*ETJ*, 1951), writing on the preoccupation with salvation in the play despite its comedic texture, began its rescue from academic oblivion. The three archetypal leading male roles—the practical man, the romantic, and the saint—are, according to Smith, crucial to an understanding of Shavian drama, for overtones of them and their final trio reappear throughout Shaw. (Edmund Wilson discussed the practical man and saint polarity in his "Bernard Shaw at Eighty" in *The Triple*

Thinkers, 1938.) A study of Shaw's playwriting techniques using *John Bull's Other Island* as model is Jere Shanor Veilleux, "Shavian Drama: A Dialectical Convention for the Modern Theatre" (*TCL*, 1958), where the dialogue is examined in terms of the Socratic pattern of contradiction. F.P.W. McDowell's "Politics, Comedy, Character and Dialectic: The Shavian World of *John Bull's Other Island*" (*PMLA*, 1967) analyzes English and Irish types and the subjects of Shaw's satire. Books on G.B.S. have continued to neglect *John Bull*, although Valency provides an informative background analysis, Morgan in a chapter on the play roughly parallels points made in the McDowell article, and Wisenthal in *The Marriage of Contraries* examines this play of opposing temperaments as the first of Shaw's "in which characters are overtly symbolic." Harold Ferrar, in "The Caterpillar and the Gracehoper: Bernard Shaw's *John Bull's Other Island*" (*Eire*, 1980), sees in the play "a complicated and passionate vision of Ireland." One of Shaw's aims was to pillory the cliché Irishman, and the most authoritative examination of his comedy in that context is Heinz Kosok's "John Bull's Other Ego: Reactions to the Stage Irishman in Anglo-Irish Drama," in *Medieval and Modern Ireland* (ed. Richard Wall, 1988).

Little research on the play's development exists in print. M. J. Sidnell (*MD*, 1968) extracts from Yeats's correspondence with Shaw and Lady Gregory over the Abbey's rejection of the play engineered by Yeats, defending less Yeats's esthetic positions than his political ones justified by the later *Playboy* hysteria, but failing in the process to understand the comic exuberance in Shaw's satire. The Sidnell article has been revised and expanded as "Hic and Ille: Shaw and Yeats" in *Theatre and Nationalism in Twentieth-century Ireland* (ed. Robert O'Driscoll, 1971), which prints seven letters from Yeats and Shaw. Meisel's chapter on Irish romance reviews *John Bull's* inheritance from (and satire on) the "stage Irishman" farce, and R. S. Nelson (*ShawR*, 1970) suggests that the prototype for the unfrocked Father Keegan was not only Shaw's friend the modernist Catholic priest George Tyrrell, who was unfrocked in 1906—after the play—but also another Shaw friend, Edward Carpenter, whose unorthodox ideas and simple life had resulted in his leaving the Anglican priesthood.

Major Barbara

One of the handicaps that has faced *John Bull's Other Island* since it was succeeded on the stage by *Major Barbara* (written 1905) is that it was closely sandwiched in time between two of Shaw's most profound and provocative dramas. More scholarship and explication of high quality has been devoted to *Major Barbara* than to any other play by G.B.S. The texts have been examined scrupulously for hints of elusive meaning to be gleaned from changes in the printed versions or the later film script and from the much more substantial alterations made in manuscript as Shaw wrote the play. And a textual note in *Notes and Queries* (1989) by Michael Von Albrecht, "Fate or Hate? A Textual Problem in Shaw's *Major Barbara*," demonstrates again, from a printer's misreading in act 2, how Shaw's texts remain less than definitive and how even minor errors garble meaning.

Crompton's chapter on the play studies it from the standpoint of Shaw's cynicism about liberal idealism and utilizes among other Shaw manuscripts the first ("Derry") manuscript of the play to define the character and philosophy of Andrew Undershaft, who is portrayed with less subtlety in the earlier text. B. F. Dukore in *Shaw the Playwright* and separate essays has also studied the manuscript and published texts, and S. P. Albert (*ETJ*, 1968) examines how act 3 was rewritten under the impetus of Gilbert Murray's criticisms and how much the play owes in characterization to Murray and the aristocratic family into which he had married. (Undershaft calls Cusins "Euripides," and in this context it is instructive to examine Gilbert Norwood's *Euripides and Shaw* [1921].) Albert also adds to the understanding of

Shaw's own perspectives toward the play in his "Shaw's Advice to the Players of *Major Barbara*" and "More Shaw Advice to the Players of *Major Barbara*" (*ThS*, 1969, 1970).

Studies of the complex origins of the play have added dimensions to its meaning. Albert has published an essay on the philosophical backgrounds of the play, "The Price of Salvation: Moral Economics in *Major Barbara*" (*MD*, 1971), and another on the real-life distillery aspect of the play, " 'Letters of Fire against the Sky': Bodger's Soul and Shaw's Pub" (*ShawR*, 1968). In "The Lord's Prayer and *Major Barbara*" (*SHAW* 1, 1981), Albert persuades us that the Lord's Prayer can be seen as an intentional and ironic gloss on the play. As does Crompton in *Shaw the Dramatist*, M. Morgan looks at the religious aspects of *Barbara* through the Nietzschean concept of Dionysius, which Shaw knew from *The Birth of Tragedy*, in "Shaw, Yeats, Nietzsche and the Religion of Art" (*Komos*, 1967). Her *Shavian Playground* chapters on the play cover similar ground. After Joseph W. Frank explored the play as religious allegory (*PMLA*, 1956), S. Weintraub supplied a corroborative "Addendum," (*ShawR*, 1958) on the Church of St. Andrew Undershaft in London and its pertinent history; and in Weintraub's "Four Fathers for Barbara," the four munitions-maker antecedents for Andrew Undershaft are related to the character and the play (*Unexpected Shaw*). Weintraub also demonstrates in "Bernard Shaw in Darkest England: G.B.S. and the Salvation Army's General William Booth" (*SHAW* 10, 1990) that Booth's 1890 polemic, which included a plan for the socioeconomic regeneration of England, is closely paralleled by Andrew Undershaft, who adopts the principles without the religion. Shaw's interest in the Salvation Army is shown to be considerable and creatively influential from as early as his first years in London.

Additional source studies of more restricted scope are J. B. Kaye's in *Shaw and Nineteenth Century Tradition*, where the Carlylean aspects of the play are identified and Undershaft seen as possibly derived from "Plugson of Undershot," owner of a firm located in the parish of St. Dolly Undershot; D. H. Bowman's

"Shaw, Stead and the Undershaft Tradition" (*ShawR*, 1971), on the Andrew Carnegie element in Barbara's industrialist father; and J. L. Wisenthal's "The Underside of Undershaft: A Wagnerian Motif in *Major Barbara*" (*ShawR*, 1972), on Shaw's equation of Alberich with industrialists of the Krupp, Cadbury, and Lever variety—and thus with Undershaft.

Critical studies of the play as theater and as literature are numerous. One of the most provocative—and unflattering—remains Francis Fergusson's chapter in *The Idea of a Theatre* (1949), "On Shavian Theatricality: The Platform and the Drawing-Room." More philosophical is Charles Frankel's "Efficient Power and Inefficient Virtue" in *Great Moral Dilemmas in Literature Past and Present* (ed. R. M. MacIver, 1956), which examines the way Shaw attempts to synthesize virtue and power. B. B. Watson's "Sainthood for Millionaires" (*MD*, 1968) takes up the same theme, seeing as Shaw's point that the world must be saved by its worldly saints and by wordly means; while B. F. Dukore (*MD*, 1966) again examines the problem of joining virtue to power, this time imaginatively via the working maxims of the six previous Andrew Undershafts as well as the laconic one ("Unashamed") of the seventh armaments czar, Barbara's father. The "Mephistopheles-Machiavelli" side of Undershaft is explained by C. A. Berst (*Art*), who points out that "In his social role Undershaft is quite like Milton's Satan, forced by circumstance to make a religion of his surroundings. He is a prose picture of the assertion that 'The mind is its own place, and in itself / Can make a Heav'n of Hell, a Hell of Heav'n.' " Shifting literary metaphors to the Blakean, Berst goes on to suggest that the denouement is a "Marriage of Heaven and Hell." Still, few explanations of the play's dramatic and intellectual effectiveness improve upon two brilliant reviews of the first production—those by Desmond MacCarthy (rpt. in his *Court Theatre* and in his *Shaw*) and Max Beerbohm (rpt. in *Around Theatres*). MacCarthy sees *Major Barbara* as "the first English play which has for its theme the struggle between two religions in one mind," and Beerbohm, in "Mr Shaw's Position," recants his own position on the stageability of Shavian drama by conceding that the Court Theatre production of *Barbara* had convinced him that he had read the plays without "theatrical imagination."

The meanings of the play continue to tantalize critics, and clearly the work has many dimensions. In "Logic and Religion in *Major Barbara*" (*MD*, 1978), Stuart E. Baker attempts a synthesis of meanings, explaining that the play, rather than being "confused or contradictory as many have claimed. . . , is a marvel of logical consistency, amazingly compact in its thorough dramatic exposition of Shaw's philosophy"; it is also "a profoundly religious play, and Major Barbara is not its only saint." J. P. Smith (*ESC*, 1978) also goes at the critical difficulties of the work, concluding that *Major Barbara* approaches "Euripidean tragedy. Given the materials with which he had chosen to work and his deep perplexity over the central moral problem of the play, not even Shaw, with all his zestful creativity and rhetoric, could turn it convincingly to comedy." B. F. Dukore's *Money and Politics in Ibsen, Shaw and Brecht* (1980) is useful on the money basis of society in *Major Barbara*, while Ken A. Baskin's "Undershaft's Challenge and the Future of the Race" (*ShawR*, 1978) draws parallels between Shaw's eugenic ideas in the play and Robert Ardrey's theories in *African Genesis* (1961).

The Doctor's Dilemma

The accepted source for *The Doctor's Dilemma* (1906), Shaw's involvement with Dr. Almroth Wright and his experiments at St. Mary's Hospital, is well known from Shaw himself. William Archer's challenge to Shaw to write a death scene is also well known; however, only in M. Quinn's "William Archer and *The Doctor's Dilemma*" (*SHAW* 4, 1984) is Archer's role spelled out and the relevant documents made available. The fifth (and final) act of the play has inspired much of the most interesting writing about it. Crompton (in *Shaw the Dramatist*) has published extracts from a BL manuscript first draft of the act as an appendix to his discussion of the backgrounds and composition of the play, and M. Morgan, in her preface to the Garland facsimile of Shaw's entire manuscript, examines what she calls "the gradual accumulation of the materials for the play in his mind," including his rehearsal notes for the Court Theatre's premiere. S. Weintraub's "A Jennifer from Australia: Edith Adams, Her Husband, and *The Doctor's Dilemma*" (*SHAW* 6, 1986) explores a G.B.S. infatuation of 1893–94 that may have been a germ of the play. Like Shaw's Jennifer, Edith also promoted the posthumous reputation of her "artist" husband (a poet), like Louis Dubedat a tubercular and unlike him a suicide.

Norbert F. O'Donnell in "Doctor Ridgeon's Deceptive Dilemma" (*ShawR*, 1959) examines Ridgeon's misunderstandings of art, love, and ethics, all three themes of the play, which lead him to assume a medical dilemma where none exists. A. Turco is similarly concerned with the legitimacy of the dilemma in "Sir Colenso's White Lie" (*ShawR*, 1970), seeing Ridgeon's "ten men in a life-boat" dilemma as moral posturing and a fabrication and the play as a black comedy in which the lovesick Ridgeon succeeds in killing his rival (for a woman) and discovers that he has—in his own words—"committed a purely disinterested murder." Dr. Ridgeon is central to J. Bertolini's "*The Doctor's Dilemma*: The Art of Self-Undoing," *SHAW* 7 (1987), rev. in *The Playwrighting Self of Bernard Shaw* (1991). Here, where Ridgeon echoes Dudgeon, "the devices that made *The Devil's Disciple* a doppelgänger play—the exchange of identities (or transfer of guilt) between Dick Dudgeon and Anthony Anderson, . . . the discovery that each man embodies the other's secret self, a self antithetical to what each man thought he was—replicate themselves in *The Doctor's Dilemma.*"

More general analyses are J. P. Smith's in *The Image of the Work* (1955), which denies, however, Ridgeon's self-interest, and M. Morgan's discussion in *The Shavian Playground*, which concludes that the play is "Shaw's tribute of loyalty to the socialist movement in all its vagaries—including the rascality of [Edward] Aveling, the suffering of Eleanor Marx, the dreams of the Pre-Raphaelites, the robust humor and power of the work of William Morris, his public dedication and private unhappiness, and the magnificence of Jane Morris at her husband's funeral—all absorbed into a remarkable aesthetic affirmation." The aesthetic element—particularly the Pre-Raphaelite aspect—absorbs E. B. Adams in "The Unscrupulous Artist" chapter of *Bernard Shaw and the Aesthetes*, where Louis Dubedat, because of his amoral love life, personal charm (both of these equally applicable to the scientist Aveling), and cynical attitude toward his patrons, is identified with Dante Gabriel Rossetti. In a sidelight on this question, S. Weintraub in *Beardsley: A Biography* (1967) suggests that Aubrey Beardsley provided Shaw with Dubedat's profession, youthful genius, and fatal illness. As for the basic situation of the play, M. Meisel sees a Shavian bow not only to Molière but to two Victorian dramatic genres, "Domestic Comedy" and "Comedy of the Professions"; and Weintraub sees (in "The Embryo Playwright") characters and situations ripening for the play in the early novels (*TSLL*, 1959).

The medical side of the drama—Shaw wryly subtitled it a tragedy, writing about doctors and medicine in general—has elicited surprisingly little serious research and criticism, although Roger Boxill has devoted an entire book, *Shaw and the Doctors* (1969), to a thorough airing of the subject. That the medical profession did not take seriously his implicit and explicit injunctions to examine and heal itself must have irritated Shaw all his life.

Getting Married

Getting Married (written 1907–8), although antedating *Blanco Posnet*, fits closely in Shaw's developing dramaturgy with the conversation comedies which followed *Blanco Posnet, Misalliance* (written 1909), and *Fanny's First Play* (written 1910–11). "The *Getting Married* Controversy" (*ShawR*, 1966) reprints the exchanges between Shaw and Lord Alfred Douglas in *The Athenaeum*, which Douglas then edited, in which Wilde's former lover expressed his moral outrage about Shaw's views on marriage and divorce. The innovative nature of Shaw's playwriting technique in the play has inspired more scholarly interest than its social heresies, although these are receiving increased attention. E. Bentley in *Bernard Shaw* (1947) examines the "disquisitory" plays from the standpoint of the structural and thematic interrelationships, seeing one of their common but less obvious characteristics as their lack of protagonist. William Sharp (*ETJ*, 1959) and Stanley J. Solomon (*ShawR*, 1962) analyze the intergration of theme and structure in Shavian discussion drama. Alan J. Downer's "Shaw's First Play" (in *Shaw: Seven Critical Essays*) contrasts the techniques of *Widowers' Houses*—in point of time Shaw's first completed play—and *Getting Married*, which he sees as "the first completely Shavian play." Conversely, M. Morgan's "The Greek Form Again: *Getting Married*" chapter of *The Shavian Playground* goes beyond the classical unities the play observes to Aristophanic burlesque, in which are discovered tenuous Shavian affinities. (Other scholars, too, have located Aristophanic elements in various Shaw plays, just as Morgan and others have also seen commedia dell'arte elements in Shaw; although it is unlikely that he was free from their direct and indirect influence, claims about their impact seem exaggerated.)

Misalliance

Misalliance has received only modest scholarly attention, although it has become since Shaw's death one of his most successful plays in revival. B. C. Rosset in *Shaw of Dublin* sees in

Misalliance more profound and disturbing biographical links with Shaw's family life in Dublin than the superficial ones observed by other biographers (often with Shaw's assistance) and suggests that Shaw may even have considered himself "daring" for having put them into print, making the play "his chief vehicle for transferring something of the fascinating drama of the Shaws of Dublin to the stage." Morgan relates elements of the play to Shaw's reading of Granville Barker's *The Madras House* in manuscript; B. F. Dukore, in "*The Madras House* Prefinished" (*ETJ*, 1972), which prints Shaw's revised third act from the (University of Texas) manuscript written by Shaw to spur Barker to complete and produce the play, observes that the relationship between plays may have been symbiotic. F. P. W. McDowell, in "Shaw's Abrasive View of Edwardian Civilization in *Misalliance*" (*ShawR*, 1980), sees a steady ironic vision informing the play and observes that it is "one of Shaw's salient qualities as a dramatist in this play to inculcate some of his values through somewhat dubious spokesmen. Each of Shaw's figures has his or her moments of insight without ceasing to be limited and amusing to the spectator."

Many of these figures have real-life prototypes, much altered to stay within the libel laws (Tarleton may be the womanizing department store entrepreneur Gordon Selfridge), but one character, Hypatia (the name, however, comes from Hypatia Bradlaugh), is seen by Robert Everding in "Bernard Shaw, Miss Alliance, and Miss Cotterill (*ELN*, 1988), to be based upon "Shaw's extraordinary relationship with the exuberant and impossible poetess."

Two studies of the impact of the young field of aviation on the play are Everding's "Bernard Shaw, *Misalliance*, and the Birth of British Aviation" and R. Weintraub's "A Parachutist Prototype for Lina" (on ballooning and stunt parachuting), both in *SHAW* 8 (1988). In a novel perspective, R. Weintraub in "Johnny's Dream: *Misalliance*," *SHAW* 7 (1987) also sees the play as best directed as well as best understood when interpreted as a daydream in which Johnny Tarleton works out his dilemmas and frustrations.

Androcles and the Lion

Androcles and the Lion (written 1912) has been analyzed primarily by researchers on Shaw's religious writings (e.g., W. S. Smith, G. Weales, Abbott, Barr). It might be said of a number of Shaw plays, but especially of *Androcles*, that the best commentary about it remains the original review by Desmond MacCarthy (*NewS* [6 September 1913], rpt. in his *Shaw*), who noted his "discovery" after seeing the first production that the playwright's "most striking" intellectual qualities "spring from his being extraordinarily free from all forms of spiritual snobbery." Its origins in Victorian Christmas pantomimes are so palpable that Meisel devotes a chapter, "Christian Melodrama and Christmas Pantomine," entirely to the play, and Berst in his *Art* observes that "conceptually" it does not matter that "in a spiritual sense the happiness at the end is bogus: [that] if the Christians' cause has gained ground, it has not gained on its own merit." The Happy Ending is poetic justice, which pantomines must have, but "in reality, the reformers are usually eaten [by the lions]." What is crucial is the interior of the parable. Little other serious study has been given to *Androcles*, although Valency finds interesting European analogues in Maeterlinck and in J. R. Planche's "fairy extravaganzas" as well as later in Anouilh. Susan Stone-Blackburn's essay (*ShawR*, 1978) examines how Shaw turned the legend as told by Aulus Gellius into philosophic farce, at the same time satirizing contemporary religious melodrama. The legend becomes the frame for a discussion play about concepts of salvation. And Nelson, in "Wisdom and Power in *Androcles and the Lion*" (*YES*, 1972), examines the play as an exploration of "genuine religious experience," while Abbott views that experience in contemporary Christian terms.

The Shewing-Up of Blanco Posnet

The seldom performed—and at first censored—*The Shewing-Up of Blanco Posnet* (written 1909), which Shaw first subtitled *A Sermon in Crude Melodrama*, is seldom studied apart from examinations of Shaw's religious plays. Valency writes that Shaw's Western frontier allegory, despite its weaknesses, "has nevertheless aroused some scholarly interest," but the nontheological interest seems centered almost entirely in Meisel's study, where each of Shaw's plays is found to have some Victorian theatrical antecedent. (The Bret Harte–David Belasco American mining camp melodramas are late nineteenth century in date but owe little to the contemporary English stage on which they sometimes appeared.) The best account of its notorious first production—in Dublin to evade the Lord Chamberlain's suppression in London—is Dan H. Laurence's (*ShawR*, 1955), which includes comments by W. B. Yeats and a review by James Joyce.

David Matual's "*The Shewing-Up of Blanco Posnet* and Tolstoy's *The Power of Darkness*: Dramatic Kinship and Theological Opposition" (*SHAW* 1, 1981) suggests that Shaw's play echoes Tolstoy's "in the details of its plot and setting," although "its theological orientation underscores the basic and irreconcilable differences between Shaw and the Russian moralist." A. Abbott's *Shaw and Christianity* attributes Blanco's conversion to his coming to an understanding "that God is real and that the reality of God is a terrifying thing." R. S. Nelson's "Blanco Posnet: Adversary of God" (*MD*, 1970) also addresses the conversion, seeing "Blanco's discovery of his place in a [purposeful] cosmic program."

Fanny's First Play

Shaw's longest first-run—and authentic hit play—*Fanny's First Play* has elicited little solid scholarship since 1912. One must begin with C. A. Carpenter's "Shaw's Cross-Section of Anti-Shavian Opinion," *ShawR* (1964), which compares the real-life London critics with their caricatures. Dukore (in *Bernard Shaw, Playwright*) is one of the few critics to comment at length on the interrelations between frame play and inner play, which present "parallel characters and situations" that yield "alternative views that illuminate each other." While he sees commedia elements in the play, Valency (*Cart and Trumpet*) sees "the Italian *grotteschi*." And Barbara Fisher in "*Fanny's First Play*: A Critical Potboiler?" (*SHAW* 7, 1987) answers her own question in the negative. Nelson's "*Fanny's First Play* and *The Mill on the Floss*" (*ShawR*, 1969) examines the core play as an ironic retelling of George Eliot, "for Shaw tells essentially the same story although he moves to a drastically different conclusion." For the background to Shaw's "prologue in pantomine doggerel" written in 1916 to shorten the play, see S. Weintraub's *Journey to Heartbreak*. (The prologue became a war casualty.)

"Tomfooleries"

Dark Lady of the Sonnets (written 1910) has little subtext to explicate; further, its origins are clear from Shaw's lengthy preface. But an entire literature exists on Shaw and Shakespeare, to be examined in a later section. A rare full examination is Sally Peters's "Shaw's Double Dethroned: *The Dark Lady of the Sonnets* . . ." (*SHAW* 7, 1987), which deals with Shaw's three overtly Shakespearean stage pieces and considers the Bard as "Shaw's darker self and . . . omnipresent father."

Shaw's other short plays written in the first two decades of the century, from curtain-raisers to—as he rightly described them—"tomfooleries," have attracted little scholarly attention, although *The Admirable Bashville* (written 1902), because of its obvious derivation from the novel *Cashel Byron's Profession*, is discussed by S. Weintraub (*TSLL*, 1959) and R. Hogan (*ELT*, 1965); and the trivial *Passion, Poison and Petrifaction* (written 1905) has been examined provocatively by Paul Silverstein in "Barns, Booths, and Shaw" (*ShawR*, 1969) not only for its own brand of satire but as an anticipation of Ionesco-like absurdism. In "Tomfooling with Melodrama," *SHAW* 7 (1987), Ina Rae Hark examines the playlet as a spoof on "the melodramatic conception of passion as jealousy [to which Shaw will not grant] any psychological privilege at all."

B. C. Rosset in *Shaw of Dublin* sees *The Fascinating Foundling, Press Cuttings* (both written 1909), and the many other plays and playlets of Shaw's in which a foundling is crucial or bastardy or doubtful parentage is involved (as in *Misalliance*) not as mere satirizing of an old plot device but as part of the playwright's compulsion to send a particular "biographical rabbit" through the "warrens" of his work—his alleged concerns about his mother's relationship with G.J.V. Lee, and thus with his own parentage. In *Fabian Feminist*, Michael Weimer's "*Press Cuttings* and Women's Suffrage" puts the play into historical context. (Shaw did indeed have censorship problems because of his thinly veiled references to living politicians.)

In "Shaw Improves Shaw" (*MD*, 1963), Dukore analyzes and compares the 1907 and 1931 texts of *How He Lied to Her Husband*, demonstrating that Shaw deleted topical allusions to early productions of *Candida* and to actors and critics. In "Bernard Shaw and *The Interlude at the Playhouse*" (*ShawR*, 1960), Myron Matlaw recounts the composition, production, and reception of the 1907 playlet. A piece that illuminates the possible impact of Shaw's 1912 farce *Overruled* upon another writer more than it elucidates the playlet itself is S. Weintraub's "A Respectful Distance: James Joyce and His Dublin Townsman Bernard Shaw" (*JML*, 1986), which demonstrates persuasive parallels between the "Juno" of Shaw's play, whom Joyce may have encountered in both English and German texts, and the Molly Bloom of *Ulysses* (written 1914–21).

In Dukore's *Playwright* the 1920–21 farce-adaptation *Jitta's*

Atonement is examined for what its many variations from Siegfried Trebitsch's original play tell us of Shaw's dramatic techniques. Myron Matlaw in *Jitta's Atonement: Shaw's Adaptation and the Translation of Trebitsch's Original* (1979) misleads in title and subtitle, since the monograph is actually a translation of Trebitsch's original *Frau Gittas Sühne*, with a preface, and does not include Shaw's very free version. S. Weintraub has described the composition (and, in some cases, production) of the wartime playlets in *Journey to Heartbreak*, observing that one of them, *Annajanska; or The Bolshevik Empress* (written 1917), is an "embryonic suggestion" of *Saint Joan*.

Pygmalion

The scholarly literature on *Pygmalion* has been stimulated mainly by controversies about Shaw's ironic unsentimental conclusion. James Melton Creel's unpublished dissertation "The Phonetic Play: *Pygmalion* from Manuscript to First Printing," *DAI* (1985) examines the shorthand manuscript and the somewhat flawed transmission of the text to typescript and printed play. General analyses of its structure have often resulted from attempts to build a case for a particular thesis about the ending of the original play, the film script, or the musical version in which Shaw had no hand, although the adapter of the latter, Alan Jay Lerner, has described its text in "*Pygmalion* and *My Fair Lady*" (*ShawR*, 1956) as having in it "sixty percent of the original play." Lerner's memoir, *The Street Where I Live* (1978), furnishes sidelights on reinterpretations of the play that occurred during the conception and production of *My Fair Lady* (1956).

Whatever Shaw's contributions to the screenplay, the stage version remains the text by which to understand Shaw's methods and motives, for the exigencies of a different medium and audience required a different (as well as ex post facto) treatment, and C. A. Berst (in *Art*) is correct to insist, in discussing the "tightness of context and economy of detail" that typify most Shavian dramatic patterns, that a good example of Shaw's "economy and aesthetic discipline is his elimination (in the pre-cinema text) of what might be the triumphal climax of *Pygmalion*—the Ambassador's party scene."

E. Bentley in his *Bernard Shaw* provides the standard analysis, perceiving the play as "a singularly elegant structure. . . . It is a good play by perfectly orthodox standards and needs no theory to defend it. It is Shavian . . . in being based on the standard conflict of vitality and system, in working out this conflict through an inversion of romance, in bringing matters to a head in a battle of wills and words, in having an inner psychological action in counterpoint to the outer romantic action, in existing on two contrasted levels of mentality, both of which are related to the main theme, in delighting and surprising us with a constant flow of verbal music and more than verbal wit." S. J. Solomon (*ETJ*, 1964) defends Shaw's ending on structural grounds—that it is not "an arbitrary imposition of the author's temperament," for Shaw could not have intended a "sentimental and one-dimensional" play. Pygmalion must lose his Galatea because he has created (beyond his expectations?) a person with "independence of spirit and vitality of mind." The misconception that Shaw sanctioned a sentimental ending for the film and took his own epilogue as "something less than serious" is explored by B. F. Dukore's " 'The Middleaged Bully and the Girl of Eighteen': The Ending They *Didn't* Film" (*ShawR*, 1971). Dukore here has had the opportunity to examine the film script, which D. P. Costello in *The Serpent's Eye* was able to reconstruct only from the printed screen version and a transcript of the sound track.

Crompton provides a comprehensive background study in his *Shaw*, emphasizing Shaw's unsentimental and unromantic characterization of Higgins. Recognizing Shaw's irony, Berst observes (in *Art*), "As Eliza misconstrues her predicament as a seduction peril, Higgins oversimplifies the situation as a fascinating experiment. The Cinderella dreams and Pamela fears have their counterpart in the Pygmalion obsession." Similarly, Crompton concludes that the insistence on having Eliza and Higgins "end as lovebirds" shows "how popular sentiment will ignore any degree of incompatibility between a man and a woman once it has entertained the pleasant fancy of mating them." Freudian analyses—supported by Shaw's own statements, in and out of the play—suggest a further complication, that Higgins's mother-complex has disabled him from marital aspirations; and Philip Weissmann, in *Creativity in the Theatre* (1965), relates the play to oedipal feelings from Shaw's own childhood and its writing to the death of Shaw's mother and his contemporaneous—and futile—erotic pursuit of Mrs. Patrick Campbell. Henry B. Richardson (*PsyR*, 1956) classifies Higgins's problem as a "Pygmalion-reaction"—the suppression of love through aesthetics. The critical controversy has been further abetted by Silver, who, despite his pathological bias in other cases, is credibly penetrating on the oedipal side of Higgins.

Pygmalion has also attracted studies of language, in particular John A. Mills in *Language and Laughter: Comic Diction in the Plays of Bernard Shaw* (1969) and Fred Mayne in *The Wit and Satire of Bernard Shaw* (1967). Joseph Saxe's *Bernard Shaw's Phonetics: A Comparative Study of Cockney Sound-Changes* (1936) is the most exhaustive on the flavorsome diction of Eliza and her father. Another perspective is provided in Hugo Beardsmore's "A Sociolinguistic Interpretation of *Pygmalion*" (*ES*, 1979), which reminds Shaw's audience, "It is language which is at the very core of the action of *Pygmalion* and indeed it would be difficult to give any other credible interpretation of the theme of this play than that of the relationship between code, personality and social class."

There are numerous accounts, anecdotal and otherwise, of the events leading up to the composition and production of *Pygmalion*, both in Shavian biographies and memoirs and in biographies of Mrs. Shaw, Mrs. Patrick Campbell, and Herbert

Beerbohm Tree. Richard Huggett's *The Truth about Pygmalion* (1970) is an entertaining journalistic potpourri of all of them.

Influence studies continue to complicate the intellectual backgrounds of *Pygmalion*, as they have ever since one critic looked behind the titular myth to see also the myth of Cinderella, and another suggested an episode in Smollett's novel *Peregrine Pickle*. Michael Goldberg's "Shaw's *Pygmalion*: The Reworking of *Great Expectations*" (*ShawR*, 1979) sees a Pygmalion-Galatea parallel in the Magwitch-Pip relationship and views the ending of *Pygmalion* as "a creative criticism of the ending of *Great Expectations*." E. F. Briden's "James's Miss Churm: Another of Eliza's Prototypes?" (*ShawR*, 1976) examines a character in Henry James's short story "The Real Thing" (1892); while Sara Moore Putzell, in "Another Source of *Pygmalion*: G.B.S. and Mrs. Braddon" (*ShawR*, 1979), points to the novel *Our Adversary* (1909, just before the play was written). T. Vesonder in *Fabian Feminist* points out that the core of both the Pygmalion myth and the Cinderella folktale is the transformation, not the marriage, which would warp the dramatic focus and merely have Eliza "trade masters—poverty and vulgarity for Higgins."

Heartbreak House

Heartbreak House (written 1916–17) is one of Shaw's most complex creations, with its origins literary and philosophical as well as rooted in actuality. Some of its history is lost because no manuscript survives, but a corrected typescript (BL), substantially longer than the published production text, is reproduced in the Garland series, ed. S. Weintraub and A. Wright (see Editions above), although *Heartbreak House* is not, chronologically, an "early text." Reviewing the play's multiple subtexts, the editors observe that the typescript supports a Trojan myth dimension suggested in the published play by names, events, and even props; for example, the original name for Hesione, Captain Shotover's elder daughter, was Hecuba. Other Homeric allusions identify pre-1914 England as "a smug and complacent Troy."

Heartbreak House is also, literally, England. A. H. Nethercot, in "Zeppelins over Heartbreak House" (*ShawR*, 1966), describes the events over Ayot St. Lawrence on the night of 30 September–1 October 1916 that provided G.B.S. with the apocalyptic climax and conclusion to the play. S. Weintraub in *Journey to Heartbreak* (1971) traces not only the development of the play but Shaw's own transition from the optimism that had generated *Pygmalion* to the despair of the war years that culminates in *Heartbreak House* and the two major plays that followed. In the process Shaw's own words in his preface to the play (1919) that "when the play was begun not a shot had been fired" and his equivalent words to Archibald Henderson quoted in *Playboy and Prophet* (1932), both of which had caused the composition of the play to be ascribed to 1913–16, are shown to be at odds with the facts. Actual writing appears to have been begun on 4 March 1916 and completed late in May 1917; but it is possible that Shaw's thoughts about the play began to form after he saw Chekhov's plays in a Moscow Art Theatre touring production in London in 1913—the inspiration for the subtitle, *A Fantasia in the Russian Manner on English Themes.* Michael J. Mendelsohn (*ShawR*, 1963) sees the play as a redistillation of *The Cherry Orchard* (and earlier Chekhov plays); while Robert Corrigan (*ShawR*, 1959) sees the play as a pessimistic view of the contemporary scene. A persuasive overview of *Heartbreak House* in the light of prewar English society is A. Wright's "*Heartbreak House*" chapter in her *Literature of Crisis* (1984), in which she observes that in the play "the chronic Condition of England becomes acute, and quite possibly terminal. In this extremity the play asks: who can save the country?" Here Shaw's drama is seen in the context of Forster's *Howards End* and Eliot's *The Waste Land* (the latter a parallel also drawn earlier by Colin Wilson but only in passing). As Wright sees it, the house is "the diminishing or crumbling centre of civilisation."

Other literary and philosophical approaches in the play are spelled out by L. Crompton in *Shaw*, where "the spirit behind *Heartbreak House*" is thought to be Old Testament–Carlylean, particularly the books of Micah, Jeremiah, and Exodus; by S. Weintraub ("Shaw's *Lear*," in *Unexpected Shaw*), who views the play as Shaw's attempt to provide a *Lear*-dimension of echoes and reverberations; and by D. J. Leary (*MD*, 1972), who sets out to show Shaw's connections with the "whole mythopoetic content of English art" with special reference to Blake. (Despite Leary's essay, the earlier essay by Fiske noted under *The Devil's Disciple*, and J. B. Kaye's *Shaw and the Nineteenth Century Tradition*, Blake's impact upon G.B.S. remains insufficiently explored.) A pregnant observation by C. Wilson in his *Bernard Shaw: A Reassessment* about the philosophical tone of the play is that it "anticipates Eliot's *Waste Land* in its tone and in its analysis of the problem of a civilization undermined by triviality and 'nihlism.' But Eliot arrived at the conclusion that the answer lies in a return to traditional Christianity, and Shaw was quite certain that it did not." In *Homage to Daniel Shays: Collected Essays 1952–1972* (1972), Gore Vidal, however, sees a curious paradox emerging from Shaw's despair. "*Heartbreak House* is a moonlight play, suitable for recapturing the past. Elegy and debate cancel one another out. Nor is the work really satiric, an attack on 'folly and worthlessness.' These people are splendid and unique, and Shaw knows it. He cannot blow them up at the end."

The dimension of actuality in the play is noted in suggestions for the prototypes of its leading characters. Crompton puts forward Mrs. Patrick Campbell for Hesione (as Shaw had confided to her), Cunninghame Graham for her husband Hector (who has also been thought to contain elements of Shaw's womanizing Fabian friend Hubert Bland), and businessman Hudson Kearley (Lord Devonport) for Boss Mangan (this also established from Shaw's correspondence). His suggestion that Shaw's idealistic city-planner friend Ebenezer Howard is the basis for the weak Liberal dreamer Mazzini Dunn seems tenuous. Weintraub adds actress Lena Ashwell's father Captain Pocock, characteristics of whom Shaw put into Captain Shotover (Julian Kaye also notes Carlyle's Plugson of Undershot), and Virginia and Leonard Woolf as the imperious Lady Ariadne Utterword and her absent colonial governor husband Sir Hastings; Weintraub also identifies the Webbs' rented country house in Sussex, Windham Croft, where the Shaws and Woolfs weekended in 1916, as the original of Heartbreak House. Richard Gill's *Happy Rural Seat: The English Country House and the Literary Imagination* (1972) places the play in the context of other treatments of the country house as metaphor for England and perceives it as announcing both symbol and theme for a new generation of writers.

A curious and indirect commentary on *Heartbreak House* is Virginia Woolf's family farce *Freshwater* (1923, rev. 1935; pub. 1976). In the earlier version James the Butler (a nonfamily role) echoes the visionary speeches of Captain Shotover, while the real-life artist George Frederic Watts evinces the baffled idealism of Mazzini Dunn, and several of the women, including Virginia's aunt, Julia Cameron, suggest Shaw's characters in what seems a burlesque on the play in which Virginia herself may have been burlesqued.

Critical perspectives have been numerous and at wide variance with one another. Stark Young's disappointed review of a thirties revival (rpt. in *Immortal Shadows*, 1938) had some influence in inhibiting productions; and Mary McCarthy's essay on the same performance (rpt. in *Sights and Spectacles*, 1956), in which she discerned "the terror of the play's lost author, who could not, in conscience, make his story come out right, or indeed, come out at all," was misunderstood at the time as being in the same vein, although its aim was to stress the ominousness in the play. Soon afterward this was understood. *Heartbreak House* found its time in the shattered world that was the legacy of World War II.

F. P. W. McDowell's "Technique, Symbol, and Theme in *Heartbreak House*," (*PMLA*, 1953) remains the standard examination of Shaw's dramatic devices, improving upon William Irvine's explication of the allegory in *The Universe of G.B.S.* A useful supplement is Michael W. Kaufman's "The Dissonance of Dialectic: Shaw's *Heartbreak House*" (*ShawR*, 1970), which analyzes the structural elements as possibly derived from the musical fantasia and sees the drama as evolving "from the decacaphony produced by the [ten] counterpointed characters. . . . Form and meaning coalesce." Both M. Morgan (in *The Shavian Playground*) and Berst (in *Bernard Shaw and the Art of Drama*) see *Heartbreak House* as a dream play—an insight that has come strikingly late to critics, since Ellie Dunn falls asleep at the beginning of the play and Hesione Hushabye (her charactonym itself should have awakened readers and viewers) dozes offstage, while Boss Mangan is put into a hypnotic sleep in a later act; and talk of sleep and dreams permeates the dialogue. The dream atmosphere helps explain the dislocations and the illogic others have seen in the play and gives weight to "mad" old Captain Shotover's cursing "the happiness of yielding and dreaming instead of resisting and doing, the sweetness of the fruit that is going rotten." The Strindbergian vein in the play has yet to be carefully examined.

Viewing the play from a theatrical angle, Harold Clurman (*TDR*, 1961) finds subtleties in characterization and meaning that may escape a purely literary reading. D. C. Coleman (*DramaS*, 1966–67) looks at the play from the perspective of a work "strikingly similar in setting and structure," Edward Albee's *Who's Afraid of Virginia Woolf?* (1962). With surprisingly little strain Coleman elaborates on his thesis that "the action of both [plays] advances by means of domestic sport, called by Albee 'fun and games.'" Thus the suggestion advanced in *Journey to Heartbreak* of a Virginia Woolf component to *Heartbreak House* becomes a strange irony.

Heartbreak House is rapidly approaching *Major Barbara* in attractiveness to exegetes. M. Quinn's "The Dickensian Presence in *Heartbreak House*" (*ShawR*, 1977) ranges through *Bleak House*, *Dombey and Son*, *David Copperfield*, *Oliver Twist*, *Little Dorrit*, and *Hard Times* for evidence of the usefulness of Dickens to Shaw;

and J. W. Frank, in "Internal vs. External Combustion: Dickens's *Bleak House* and *Heartbreak House*" (*ShawR*, 1977), sees further evidence of the pervasive impact of Dickens. Sally Peters Vogt (*MD*, 1978) views *Heartbreak House* as a statement on the future of England in two metaphors—the ship of state and the ship of fools. A. Wright, in "Shaw's Burglars: *Heartbreak House* and *Too True to Be Good*" (*ShawR*, 1980), argues that Shaw saw burglars as symbolic of those classes who live on unearned income and thus represent the worst aspects of capitalist society. Fred E. Stockholder (*ShawR*, 1976) analyzes the play's thought as deriving from the philosophical pessimism not only of Nietzsche but also of Schopenhauer, while Thomas R. Whitaker, in "Dreaming the Music," in his *Fields of Play in Modern Drama* (1977), elicits meaning from the work's performance qualities, seeing a paradox of "rhetorical puppets" with "a surprisingly rich vitality." James Woodfield's "Ellie in Wonderland: Dream and Madness in *Heartbreak House*" (*ESC*, 1985) parallels the 1985 Shaw Festival (Canada) production of the play in using *Alice in Wonderland* as a point of departure, since "a fluidity of form . . . reconcile[s] the contradictions of tragedy and comedy and of sanity and madness."

Back to Methuselah

The five-play cycle *Back to Methuselah* (written 1917–20) is likely to generate more research and criticism than almost any other Shavian play; the aggregate, however, is currently small. The beginnings of research into Shaw's sources were in H. M. Geduld's six-volume variorum edition of the play submitted as a doctoral thesis at Birkbeck College, University of London (1961). From it Geduld has drawn three useful articles: "The Textual Problem in Shaw" (*ShawR*, 1962) concerns the need to reconcile changes made silently in subsequent printings of the play as well as to correct errors in the American editions G.B.S. did not proof. "The Lineage of Lilith" (*ShawR*, 1964) seeks to explain where Shaw sought his information on the apocryphal character who appears only in the final pages of "As Far as Thought Can Reach" (the fifth play in the cycle) and his motives in introducing her "during the last moments before the final curtain." Geduld also provides a useful stage history of the first performances in England (*MD*, (1959), including newspaper accounts, letters, and reminiscences of participants. (L. Langner's *The Magic Curtain* and *G.B.S. and the Lunatic* detail the American opening from the perspective of the Theatre Guild management.) B. G. Knepper's "*Back to Methuselah* and the Utopian Tradition" (diss., Nebraska, 1967) relates the play to the utopias of Plato, More, Swift, and Bulwer-Lytton, the latter material published by Knepper as "Shaw's Debt to the Coming Race" (*JML*, 1971). This science fiction aspect of *Methuselah*, its origins, and its impact on subsequent writers in the genre, is the major, although not the only, theme of scholars in the "Shaw and Science Fiction" issue of *ShawR* (ed. J. R. Pfeiffer, 1973).

Back to Methuselah continues to intrigue science fiction advocates as well as its more likely audience. Pfeiffer's *Back to Methuselah* entry in the encyclopedic five-volume *Survey of Science Fiction Literature* (vol. 1, 1979) emphasizes the science fiction aspects, while two other essays suggest the play's continuing science fiction impact. John Aquino's "Shaw and C. S. Lewis's *Space Trilogy*" (*ShawR*, 1975) maintains that Lewis, despite his dislike of Shaw, was indebted to *Methuselah*, while composer Michael Tippett's "*Back to Methuselah* and *The Ice Break*" (*ShawR*, 1978) acknowledges that *Heartbreak House* and, especially, the last play in the *Methuselah* cycle influenced his science fiction opera.

That Shaw may have received his ideas about death resulting from "discouragement" in "The Tragedy of an Elderly Gentleman" (IV) from Sir Francis Galton as well as from Bulwer-Lytton is one of the theses advanced by Crompton in *Shaw the Dramatist*;

while W. S. Smith (*ShawR*, 1975), analyzes "Tragedy" and death by "discouragement" by basing his perspective on Alvin Toffler's concept of "future shock." J. W. Frank (*ShawR*, 1976) sees the bleak play as Sophoclean in its grandeur, Shaw's *Oedipus at Colonus.* Two literary perspectives are F. D. Crawford's "Shaw among the Houyhnhnms" (*ShawR*, 1976), which sees the fourth play as Shaw's equivalent to the fourth part of Swift's *Gulliver's Travels*, a commentary on the inferiority of contemporary man; and V. Rao's "*Back to Methuselah*: A Blakean Interpretation" (*SHAW* 1, 1981), which continues her study in progress of the profound Blakean impact on Shaw's work. (An earlier portion of this work is cited under *Mrs Warren's Profession:* D. J. Leary, it should be noted, examined *Heartbreak House* through a Blakean lens in *MD*, 1972.)

M. Morgan in "*Back to Methuselah*: The Poet and the City" (*Shavian Playground*) analyzes the cycle largely in terms of Plato's *Republic* and Swift's *Gulliver's Travels*, cautioning that "Once we cease to be deluded by the fable of longevity," which serves only as a vehicle for the play's essential structure, the cycle becomes not a "straggling chronicle-play" but a "total image of man." The only useful study of mythic elements in the play is Richard Foster and D. J. Leary's "Adam and Eve: Evolving Archetypes in *Back to Methuselah*" (*ShawR*, 1961). S. Weintraub's *Journey to Heartbreak* traces the use of contemporary people and events and the evolution of the play from idea to four-play cycle and then to five-play cycle. As Shaw often pointed out, he was the best authority on himself, and the long preface to the play, incorporating elements from lectures and lay sermons delivered as early as 1906, remains the most important critical commentary. It is supplemented by Shaw's 1944 Postscript to the Oxford World's Classics edition of the play (1945). Several of the addresses that enunciated the theories Shaw would dramatize are printed in W. S. Smith's *The Religious Speeches of Bernard Shaw* and Dan H. Laurence's *Platform and Pulpit*, and extracted in *Journey to Heartbreak.*

While the gamut of early critical opinion about the play in performance is sampled in T. F. Evans's *Critical Heritage* volume, the best evaluation of the play as a piece of theater based upon a more recent production, the Shaw Festival staging of 1986, is F. P. W. McDowell's "Some Reflections on *Back to Methuselah* in Performance," *SHAW* 8 (1988). However uneven, McDowell concludes, the cycle will be recognized through further productions as a masterly work that "challenges rather than alienates a receptive audience."

Saint Joan

Saint Joan (written 1923) has inspired a considerable critical literature. Its initial reception and performance history have been documented in detail. Alice Griffin (*ShawR*, 1955) extracts press reaction to the first New York production and two subsequent revivals, and Irving McKee (*Shavian*, 1964) also surveys the 1923–24, 1936, and 1939 American productions. E. J. West (*QJS*, 1954) reviews English as well as American productions and critiques, D. C. Gerould (*ShawR*, 1964) examines French press reaction to the Paris premiere in 1925 in addition to the continuing reputation and influence of the play in France.

Fidelity to or departure from history, chronicle, legend, and religion in the play has been scrutinized from a variety of perspectives. An early attacker was Shaw's old friend John Mackinnon Robertson, once a declared "Rationalist," who disputed the veracity of Shaw's portrayal in a small and small-minded book, *Mr. Shaw and "The Maid"* (1925) and was upheld by T. S. Eliot (*Criterion* 1926)—an ironic position in light of Eliot's later, self-confessed cribbing from *Saint Joan* for his *Murder in the Cathedral.* A denunciation similar to Robertson's was published by another Shaw friend, Charles Sarolea, as "Has Mr. Shaw Understood Joan of Arc?" (*English Review*, 1926), where Shaw is accused of creating a brilliant play by turning a pious, mystical maid into a heretic; while J. van Kan (*FortR*, 1925) denies that

Joan could be considered a premature Protestant. The best-balanced and most informed early analysis of Shaw's treatment of the historical Joan was that of the Dutch medieval historian Johan Huizinga, originally in *De Gids* (1935) and later in English translation in *Men and Ideas* (1959). "The task that Shaw has set himself," Huizinga observes, "approximates the highest task the human mind has succeeded, a few times, in accomplishing: the creation of tragedy from history."

Studies of the play as history include Hans Stoppel's examination of assertive mystics (*ES*, 1955) and William Searle's "Shaw's Saint Joan as 'Protestant' " (*ShawR*, 1972), the latter describing Joan as "irrationalist" and "quite as much of an absolutist as her judges." Crompton reviews the historical sources Shaw appears to have used in addition to the T. Douglas Murray translation of Quicherat's transcription of the trial records, making a strong case for the *Catholic Encyclopaedia* (1910) section on "Inquisition" as the basis for the Inquisitor's rationalizations. A cautionary approach to *Saint Joan* and sainthood from the standpoint of contemporary production is Albert Bermel's "The Virgin as Heretic" in *Contradictory Characters* (1973), which warns that overly reverent direction has been turning what Shaw had written into an "anti-Shaw play. . . . If the play is to have its effect, the audience must feel the force of Joan as Shaw conceived it. To start with, they must take her as a nuisance. A heroic nuisance, to be sure, . . . but a fanatical woman who gives her friends and enemies alike no peace." The most provocative piece of writing on *Saint Joan* is a short story by Michael Ayrton, "A Performance of *Saint Joan*," in his collection, *Fabrications* (1972). It imagines a wartime (1940) provincial performance of the play in which Gilles de Rais ("Bluebeard"), angry with Shaw's portrayal of him, returns to play himself in Scene II.

The play as tragedy—classical, modern, or "Shavian"—has been the subject of many studies. John Fielden sums up the evidence (*TCL*, 1957), concluding that the playwright aimed at classical tragedy, while Louis Martz (in *Tragic Themes in Western*

Literature, 1955) maintains that although this may have been Shaw's intention, he reaches only "the very rim of tragedy." However, S. J. Solomon (*MD*, 1964) defines the play not in Aristotelian terms but as pre-Brechtian "epic tragedy," explaining that "The chronicle structure becomes necessary to the epic play in order to build up *both* forces of contention to formidable size, not just to increase the hero's reputation. . . . The scope of the material handled in the epic play is generally of greater social significance than that of the tragedy, which is generally concerned with the fall of a single person."

Other studies of Shaw's attitudes toward tragedy lean heavily upon his principles in the Preface to *Saint Joan* and his practice in the play. Sylvan Barnet, in "Bernard Shaw on Tragedy" (*PMLA*, 1956), questions whether Shaw's Life Force concept is compatible with the ideas of tragedy. Critics examining the play as tragedy inevitably point to Shakespearean models as well as Greek ones, Shaw himself observing the need to save the Maid from the Bard's scurrilous and jingoistic portrayal of her as a witch. Here Frederick S. Boas's "Joan of Arc in Shakespeare, Schiller, and Shaw" (*SQ*, 1951) is an authoritative expansion of Shaw's own prefatory remarks on the subject.

B. F. Tyson's *The Story of Shaw's Saint Joan* (1982) analyzes the play's composition from the surviving shorthand manuscripts. How the idea to write a Saint Joan play matured in Shaw is the subject of S. Weintraub's "The Genesis of *Joan*," in *Unexpected Shaw*; and his "Bernard Shaw's Other Saint Joan" (*SAQ*, 1965) illuminates a living prototype, T. E. Lawrence, whose person and personality intruded into Shaw's life the year the play was written. Shaw's state of mind as he prepared the play for production is best seen in L. Langner's *G.B.S. and the Lunatic* (1963), where a chapter details Shaw's long-distance involvement in the first production of the play (by the Theatre Guild in New York), with much useful biographical and background material, including Shaw letters and cables.

Shaw's writing of a film version in the 1930s is the subject of the introduction to *Saint Joan: A Screenplay* (ed. B. F. Dukore,

1968), which includes the full text as well as alternative matter. Attempted censorship of the script led to Shaw's withdrawal from the project. (The film was finally produced posthumously, with a grotesquely warped script by Graham Greene, whose theology apparently was passport to noncensorship.) Shaw's own protest, "*Saint Joan* Banned: Film Censorship in the United States," appeared in the *New York Times* (1936) and the *London Mercury* (1936). Harry W. Rudman provides a survey of the film censorship problem as it related to Shaw (*ShawR*, 1958).

Several cogent critiques avoid compartmentalizing the play. Edmund Wilson's early review of the published play ("Bernard Shaw since the War," *The New Republic*, 27 August 1924) observes that "what is unexpected in Shaw" is that "we find the forces of tradition and authority represented as equally intelligent and morally admirable with the heretic and rebel" and not left with "the reassuring inference that the catastrophe of Joan—like the disillusionment of Major Barbara or the embitterment of Vivie Warren—is merely a sacrifice which will bear fruit in a more intelligent program of social reconstruction." Desmond MacCarthy's review of the London premiere (rpt. in his *Shaw*) notes "the force and fairness with which the case of her opponents is put" as well as "the startling clarity with which each one states it"; and "the intensity of its religious emotion and the grasp the playwright shows of the human pathos of one who is filled with it, as well as . . . her immunity from requiring anything like pity." An unusual reaction to the New York opening—primarily because of its source, another major playwright—was that of Luigi Pirandello, who wrote in the *New York Times Sunday Magazine* (13 January 1924) of the "half-humorous melancholy which is peculiar to the disillusioned idealist. Shaw has always had too keen a sense of reality not to be aware of the conflict between it and his social and moral ideals."

Criticism from the start has often fixed upon the relevance of the Epilogue, about which even some of Shaw's admirers have complained, William Irvine (in *Universe*) labeling it "a vulgarization and a lengthy elucidation of the obvious." But among the most persuasive later appraisals of the play is that of G. Weales in *Religion in Modern English Drama* (1961), who includes a staunch defense of the Epilogue, with its ambivalences and ironies, as the "heart" of the drama, dependent "for its irony on the Shavian assumption that Joan's death is an unnecessary horror. Yet for Joan the Catholic, her death is not a misfortune, but a triumph." J.I.M. Stewart's Shaw chapter in *Eight Modern Writers* (1963) considers *Joan* "conceivably the finest and most moving English drama since *The Winter's Tale* or *The Tempest.*" And A. N. Kaul in *The Action of English Comedy: Studies in the Encounter of Abstraction and Experience from Shakespeare to Shaw* (1970)—in effect a response to Martz—sees *Joan* as "the tragedy of an historical hero rather than a saint." Some critics have complained of lapses in taste in Shaw's biblically cadenced prose poetry, particularly where Joan is given lines allegedly too sophisticated for a young country girl. (This is criticism better applied to a realistic or naturalistic play.) The most apt response appears to be that of Arthur Mizener in "Poetic Drama and the Well-Made Play" (*English Institute Essays 1949*, 1965), where *Saint Joan* is described as having—"like the work of all great poets—the inexhaustible fascination of thought and feeling dramatically suspended in a controlled medium. . . . Every great moment in the play echoes the whole play, exactly as do the great moments in a poem."

W. Searle's *The Saint and the Skeptics: Joan of Arc in the Work of Mark Twain, Anatole France and Bernard Shaw* (1976) elaborates on the work of comparison that Shaw began himself in his preface. M. A. Cohen (*ShawR*, 1977) contends that Shaw's handling of Cauchon in the trial scene is historically false and that the character is idealized—although more a "villain" than Shaw will allow—to permit him to act tragically in the passion of his righteousness. J. A. Bertolini's "Imagining *Saint Joan*" (*SHAW* 3, 1983; revised in *The Playwrighting Self*) analyzes subtleties of meaning in the play's visual values.

Interesting special approaches include that of S. John Macksoud and Ross Altman (*QJS*, 1971), who analyze the play's dialogue according to the principles of Kenneth Burke's *Philosophy of Literary Form* to explain how Shaw succeeds in "making the audience tolerant of heresy." From the rhetorical to the political is a small jump. Alick West in *A Good Man Fallen among Fabians* sees Joan through a Marxist lens, finding the saint of the Epilogue a violation of the revolutionary spirit of the first six scenes. A. Ussher in the perspicacious *Three Great Irishmen: Shaw, Yeats, Joyce* (1952) sees Joan as "an anticipation of the superhumanity which, in Shaw's biological vision, is to replace man in an unforeseeable future. She is an unhappy Trotskyist—whose place, unfortunately, is before the Stalinist firing squads." Yet the play, paradoxically, had been highly successful in print and and performance in Russia, Anna Obraztsova very likely echoing the Soviet position in her *Dramaturgicheskii metod Bernarda Shou* (1965)—that Joan, coming from the lower orders, is "a people's heroine," with "her strength as the strength of the people, and her reason as the reason of the people." A convenient gathering of such useful criticism and research is *Saint Joan Fifty Years After: 1923/24–1973/74* (ed. S. Weintraub, 1973), which includes a number of the critiques noted above as well as other approaches to the play. Holly Hill's *Playing Joan: Actresses on the Challenge of Shaw's Saint Joan* (1987) gathers performance perspectives from actresses who have played Joan, offering insights from Siobhan McKenna, Joan Plowright, Janet Suzman, Judi Dench, Elizabeth Bergner, Wendy Hiller, Uta Hagen, and others, several of whom were coached by Shaw.

A start toward textual study of *Saint Joan* is made in the Bobbs-Merrill edition of the play (ed. S. Weintraub) with the first page of the Preface, where the editor notes that Shaw, after referring in the first (1924) printing to "obscure heroines who have disguised themselves as men to serve as soldiers," silently substituted for one of them (in the fifth impression)—the "Chevalier d'Eon"—a reference instead to the even more obscure Catalina de Erauso. Shaw had discovered that the Chevalier, a French secret agent, was actually a man who, depending on the assignment, dressed as either man or woman, but who had been thought by the English to be a woman. A minor matter, yet it is another indication—witness Redmond's note on *Man and Superman* and von Albrecht's on *Major Barbara*—that Shaw's published texts need closer scrutiny.

The Apple Cart

The Apple Cart (written 1928) broke a long playwriting hiatus for Shaw and was a major box office success, despite the mixed press that has continued through each revival. Although the first of Shaw's full-length political fantasies, it was preceded by the highly political and controversial *Gospel of the Brothers Barnabas* in the *Methuselah* cycle, which mixed political prophecy and satire with immediate postwar reality. That *The Apple Cart*, too, had its origin in the wartime atmosphere of 1914–18 is observed by S. Weintraub in *Journey to Heartbreak*; while G. Wellwarth in "Gattie's Glass of Water" (*ShawR*, 1969) expands our knowledge of the man after whom Shaw's "Breakages, Ltd." concept in the play was fashioned, Shaw having identified Alfred Gattie and told part of the story in his preface. A possible source for the play in another play is the subject of M. Morgan's "Two Varieties of Political Drama: *The Apple Cart* and Granville Barker's *His Majesty*" in *The Shavian Playground.* Most critiques emphasize the political drama. Henry J. Donahy in "*The Apple Cart*: A Chestertonian Play" (*ShawR*, 1968) sees the work as a satire on parliamentary democracy much as G.K.C. might have written it, while Gibbs sees the play as the first in a series in which Shaw would pillory the pretensions of parliamentary democracy and votes for everybody. W. S. Smith's "The Search for Good Government: *The Apple Cart, On the Rocks*, and *Geneva*" (*ShawR*, 1978) picks up a line of study that will inevitably be pursued further—that few questions were as important to Shaw as "the Platonic one of what constitutes good government. That is perhaps why until the very late years all his plays skirt the problem." Silver's *Darker Side* sees the play perversely as an attempt (through the "Orinthia" interlude scene) to humiliate Mrs. Patrick Campbell publicly, while C. A. Berst, in his provocative "Shaw, Molly Tompkins, and Italy, 1921–1950," in *SHAW* 5, *Shaw Abroad* 1985, suggests that Shaw's 1920s infatuation with the American actress had much to do with reviving the stirrings dramatized in the Interlude scene. As for Mrs. Campbell's dispute with Shaw over what she felt were clear references to her, M. Peters has extracted suppressed passages from their published correspondence in "Shaw vs. Stella: The Battle of 'The Apple Cart' " (*Harvard Magazine*, 1984) and in her *Mrs Pat.*

Reliable criticism of the play is rare, as most books on Shaw's dramaturgy close with *Saint Joan* and few critiques appear in the journals. As a result Edmund Wilson's paragraphs in "Bernard Shaw at Eighty" (*The Triple Thinkers*) remain valuable, as do Eric Bentley's in his *Bernard Shaw*; among later studies, McDowell's " 'The Eternal against the Expedient': Structure and Theme in Shaw's *The Apple Cart*" (*MD*, 1959) expertly relates the play to earlier Shavian themes and shows how the developing new themes are dramatized with "technical dexterity and dialectical skill."

Among the more curious pieces on *The Apple Cart*, more a footnote to the play than criticism, is Lord Altrincham's "Reflections on *The Apple Cart*" (*National and English Review*, 1958), which examines Shaw's political views and speculates on what would have happened had King Edward VIII adopted King Magnus's strategy with his ministers in 1936.

Too True to Be Good

The making of *Too True to Be Good* (written 1931) is described in S. Weintraub's *Private Shaw and Public Shaw* (1963), where "Private Shaw"—T. E. Lawrence—is shown to have had a direct hand in the development of the "Private Meek" role, which travesties his service situation. Weintraub's "The Two Sides of 'Lawrence of Arabia': Aubrey and Meek" (*ShawR*, 1964) supplements the findings in *Private Shaw* by explaining *Too True* as in part an analysis of Lawrence's motives and nature, which both he and G.B.S. understood to represent T.E.L.'s duality, with Meek the surface image and Aubrey Bagot the deeply disturbed inner T.E.L. Both N. O'Donnell (*PMLA*, 1957) and E. E. Stokes (*ShawR*, 1965) examine John Bunyan as a major force in Shaw's intellectual development—with special reference to *Too True* (with its Bunyanesque Sergeant), where Stokes sees Shaw giving Bunyan contemporary application, while O'Donnell sees Shaw as "Shavianizing" Bunyan to "present his own views under the guise of championing those of others." Another Shaw-Bunyan study of note is Scott McMillin's (*ShawR*, 1966), a close study of a copy of *The Life and Death of Mr Badman* "with copious annotations in Shaw's hand."

Too True has been given short shrift by critics, although revivals have demonstrated a stageability and relevance not apparent to its earliest reviewers. A useful extended analysis of the play is McDowell's " 'The Pentecostal Flame' and 'the Lower Centers' " (*ShawR*, 1959), which explains the apparently diffuse comedy as evidence of Shaw's increasing interest in stylization yet sees it as a dramatic unity, belying the assertion of the Microbe at the close of the first act that, although the play was now over, the characters would discuss it for two more acts. More narrowly focused is D. J. Leary's "*Too True to Be Good* and Shaw's Romantic Synthesis: A Religion for Our Times" (*SHAW* 1, 1981). An explanation of the play's "absurd" ending, and other advanced techniques Shaw utilizes, appears in S. Weintraub's "The Avant-Garde Shaw: *Too True to Be Good* and Its Predecessors," in *The Unexpected Shaw*, while Dukore's *Bernard Shaw, Playwright* also examines the play's structural qualities. In a shrewd chapter on Shaw in his *British and Irish Political Drama in the Twentieth Century: Implicating the Audience* (1986), D. I. Rabey analyzes the "underrated" *Too True* as in the line of Shavian plays beginning with *Misalliance* that deal with "problems of wealth." And he notes, too, that *Too True*'s "moral anarchy, black humour and grotesque fantasy frequently anticipate the tone of Howard Brenton and Howard Barker's political comic nightmares."

Village Wooing and *The Six of Calais*

Little of consequence can be noted regarding two one-act Shavian plays of the early 1930s, *Village Wooing* (written 1933) and *The Six of Calais* (written 1934). "*Village Wooing*: A Call for Individual Regeneration," by R. Everding, in *SHAW* 7 (1987), is the only substantial study of the playlet in performance, and includes a stage history. The play itself, Everding concludes, concerns "spiritual illness" and "our potential to rearrange ourselves." S. Weintraub in *Journey to Heartbreak* observes that *The Six of Calais* owes its origins to Shaw's journey to Flanders in 1917 as a war correspondent; and in "Exploiting Art" (in *The Unexpected Shaw*) he examines the playlet's relationship to Auguste Rodin's sculpture *The Burghers of Calais*.

On the Rocks

On the Rocks (written 1933), although seldom performed, has elicited a considerable but only fitfully illuminating bibliography, McDowell calling it (*ETJ*, 1961), almost alone, "one of the more satisfying of Shaw's later plays" and "a coda to *Heartbreak House*." On the other hand, Paul Hummert (in *Bernard Shaw's Marxian Romance*) sees Marxist thinking as so predominant "that the great playwright even sacrifices his usually fine dramaturgy to economics, resulting in a poor but important play," indeed the "most cynical and vicious of Shaw's plays." Few other critiques of the play apart from general assessment of the political extravaganzas of this period of Shaw's output merit note; and among general books on Shavian drama only the "Eschatological Plays" chapter of Morgan's *Shavian Playground* covers this period with any thoroughness, Morgan ending with the striking Genet-like concept of a "true perception" inherent in the political plays from *The Apple Cart* through the 1930s—"that the power enjoyed by leaders of men is like an actor's power, equally dependent on a public stage and the imaginative investment of massed humanity in the figures that perform on it. This is not only the culmination of Shaw's long concern with idealism; it is the furthest reach of his understanding of the relation of his own identity as dramatist to his political mission: that he had come to understand political realities as themselves forms of theatre; and to see the fate of democracy, and humanity's control of its own destiny, as dependent on men's understanding of the determining part that the audience plays in the theatrical event."

The Simpleton of the Unexpected Isles: A Vision of Judgment

The Simpleton of the Unexpected Isles: A Vision of Judgment (written 1934), is in its setting the product of a Shaw voyage to New Zealand and India. Its eugenic and apocalyptic thesis, the culmination of the interwar years of despair, has been seen largely as a failure, Shaw even replying to the assertion of Joseph Wood Krutch in "Shaw for Shaw's Sake," in *The Nation* (6 March 1935) that the play was meaningless vaudeville, like other then-recent Shaw plays, with a lengthy rejoinder in the *Malvern Festival Book* (1935; rpt. E. J. West's *Shaw on Theatre* and the Bodley Head Shaw, vol. 6). McDowell (*MD*, 1960) sees the play as lacking "an adequate center—a commanding protagonist"—but finds a coherence to the whole in the form of an "ideological rather than a purely dramatic organization." D. J. Leary also visualizes the play as more a drama of ideas than anything else Shaw had yet put on the stage. He describes the play (*ETJ*, 1972) as "a dialectic of inept evolution and allegorical timelessness. The synthesis . . . is not despair but an open-ended Nothing."

Utilizing a different angle of vision, M. Morgan in a chapter of *Shavian Playground*, "The Eschatological Plays," on the "extravaganzas" of the 1930s, offers one of the lengthiest considerations of *Simpleton*. In her view Shaw has turned to "the eighteenth-century literary conventions of the oriental fable." Although Shaw "focuses on an end and a failure, his play is an indication of the [Shavian] philosophy in progress. For it is informed with the commonsense recognition that the life of the prosperous, educated, humane English middle class *has* been lived in a garden of man's designing from which many natural terrors have been banished. . . ." R. S. Nelson, in "*The Simpleton of the Unexpected Isles*: Shaw's Last Judgment," *QQ* (1969), sees the allegorical message as, "What ultimately matters is the degree to which individual men cooperate with life's purposes in the development of the coming race." The Day of Judgment comes for those who fail the test. M. Martin looks at the New Zealand dimension in *SHAW* 5 (1985), while in the same volume (*Shaw Abroad*), in "Seeking the Unknowable: Shaw in India," V. Rao sees in the play Shaw's adaptation of what he has learned from Indian places and ideas, from the Jain religion and the Elephanta caves and their life-celebrating sculptures. "A major concern of *The Simpleton* is indicated in the conversation between Pra and Prola and Lady Farwaters: the gulf between the two ways of viewing God, one involving an appreciation of the life-force, . . . such as Shaw found in the Elephanta caves . . . , the other involving an adoration of the physical without the spiritual: the first may be defined as true religion, the second as idolatry."

Millionairess

The ebullient *Millionairess* (written 1932–34), subtitled "A Jonsonian Comedy," has, surprisingly, been examined in print only glancingly from the standpoint of Jonsonian comedy and in fact hardly examined at all. (A long aside in Albert H. Silverman's fine "Bernard Shaw's Shakespeare Criticism," *PMLA*, 1957, looks at the play as Jonsonian "moralistic satire.") The earliest useful examination appears in Katherine Gatch's "The Last Plays of Bernard Shaw: Dialectic and Despair," in *English Institute Essays* (1954), repr. in *English Stage Comedy* (ed. W. M. Wimsatt, Jr., 1954): "in *The Millionairess*, the familiar Shavian dialectic takes on larger dimensions. The synthesis is no longer a fusion of classes. It is no less than the vision of one world in the union of East and West." S. Weintraub looks at its relationship to Shaw's novel *Cashel Byron's Profession* in "Embryo Playwright . . . ," *TSLL* (1959); and M. Morgan in *Shavian Playground* sees Epifania's unhappiness as a romantic sickness entirely separate from the sickness of capitalism explored through her experience. On the other hand, M. Peters in "*The Millionairess*: Capitalism Bankrupt?" (*SHAW* 7, 1987), writes that Epifania discovers that while making money comes easy to her, "there is another will in the world besides her own. . . . There is no guarantee the woman who has been society's boss can become its servant . . . , [but] Shaw does offer the possibility."

Although critics should have been teased by the curious existence of two endings for the play (both printed), one for communist countries and another (the standard conclusion) for noncommunist countries, this oddity has provoked little discussion. Dukore, in *Bernard Shaw, Playwright*, observes that Shaw in his old age thus had done "what his Marxist critics had since virtually the beginning of his career asked him to do, provide an upbeat ending." But his earlier stratagems prove by this experiment to have been "artistically far more rewarding." Hummert's *Shaw's Marxian Romance* ignores the perverse alternative ending and devotes its *Millionairess* space to a discussion of the pro-Mussolini "Preface on Bosses," and Marianne Bosch in "Mother, Sister and Wife in *The Millionairess*" (*SHAW* 4, 1984) suggests that the weak men dominated by a powerful heroine reflect family background and unconscious needs.

Shakespearean Plays

The relatively minor *Cymbeline Refinished* (written 1936), Shaw's provision of an alternative ending for one of Shakespeare's last successful plays, has evoked scholarly interest because of its associations with the Bard and with critical controversies concerning Shaw's ambivalent attitudes toward him. In *Studies in Honor of T. W. Baldwin* (ed. Don Cameron Allen, 1958), Rudolph Stamm reviews the history of Shaw's attitudes toward the play and toward contemporary performances, including correspondence about the Irving (Lyceum) production with Ellen Terry, concluding with an assessment of the "refinishing" and of Shaw's virtues and limitations as a Shakespeare critic. (He treats the latter aspect more fully in *SJW*, 1958.) Earlier E. J. West had examined the "refinishing" from approximately the same angles (*TA*, 1950), using the same background material but analyzing the Shavian fifth act in greater detail. Dukore, in *Bernard Shaw, Playwright*, has also compared the original with the suggested replacement, concluding that Shaw's abridgments and alterations are "in order to make the action less unbelievable, and this negative phrase is purposeful. In comedy the preposterous may be accepted if treated as obviously comic." Leary's "Shaw versus Shakespeare: The Refinishing of *Cymbeline*" (ETJ, 1978) uses the act of "refinishing" as "a paradigm of Shaw's love/hate struggle with Shakespeare, a struggle that profoundly influenced all Shaw's major plays." J. L. Wisenthal in "Having the Last Word: Plot and Counterplot in Bernard Shaw" (*ELH*, 1983), discussing a number of Shaw works, observes that his ending to *Cymbeline* leaves the audience, as part of a deliberate dramatic strategy, "with a feeling of dissatisfaction; the discords have not been harmoniously resolved. . . ."

Edwin Wilson anthologizes the *Cymbeline* material—reviews, letters, and the act itself—in *Shaw on Shakespeare* (1961), which includes all the major (and much of the minor) Shavian statements on the Bard with the exception of the seventy-eight manuscript pages of an 1884 lecture to Furnivall's New Shakespeare Society on *Troilus and Cressida*, since published in the "Shaw/Shakespeare" issue of *ShawR* (1971). This issue also includes critiques and a useful Shaw-Shakespeare bibliographical checklist by John Rodenbeck. Jerry Lutz's thin *Pitchman's Melody: Shaw about "Shakespear"* (1974) concludes, unsurprisingly, that for Shaw—missionary and progenitor of the new drama—Shakespeare was "the means, not end." Three Bard-related plays are dealt with in "Shaw's Double Dethroned: *The Dark Lady of the Sonnets*, *Cymbeline Refinished*, and *Shakes versus Shav*," by Sally Peters, in *SHAW* 7 (1987). *Shakes versus Shav* becomes "a symbolic reordering of key materials of Shavian biography."

Finally, there is "Determinism and Voluntarism in Shaw and Shakespeare," by Friedhelm Denninghaus (*ShawR*, 1976, translated by John J. Weisert from Denninghaus's *Die dramatische Konzeption George Bernard Shaws*, Stuttgart, 1971). Shaw's characters, Denninghaus contends, "do not make history but are shaped by history," while Shakespeare "conceives of the social action as the direct consequence of personal actions."

Geneva

Geneva (written and revised 1936–38; further revised 1946) was Shaw's last play about contemporary politics, one that embroiled him in controversy not only with the critics but with Theatre

Guild director Lawrence Langner. Langner published his side of the story and his exchange of letters with Shaw (which led Shaw to rewrite parts of the play that Langner—with reason—found offensive) in *The Magic Curtain* (1951). An entire monograph-length study has been published on the play, G. A. Pilecki's *Shaw's "Geneva"* (1965), which examines the evolution of the text through its successive revisions (to keep up with affairs in Europe). Susan C. Stone (*ShawR*, 1973) attempts to disprove charges that in the play Shaw drew an apologia for strongmen in his belief that they were a necessary (and temporary) expedient en route to the Superman or the ideal society of the future. To Stone, the Hitler, Mussolini, and Franco figures are antiheroes—defective dictators, uncurbed because our social institutions are stagnant and powerless.

"*Geneva* is as close to Aristophanic comedy as any Shaw play gets," Morgan has written in *Shavian Playground.* "The fact may be connected with the publication in 1933 of [his friend] Gilbert Murray's *Aristophanes*, dedicated to G.B.S." Aristophanic tendencies in Shaw long predating the Murray book are seen in Robert R. Speckhard's two studies, "Shaw and Aristophanes: How the Comedy of Ideas Works" (*ShawR*, 1965) and "Shaw and Aristophanes: Symbolic Marriage and the Magical Doctor/Cook in Shavian Comedy" (*ShawR*, 1966); however, these do not invalidate the thesis that additional Aristophanic impetus may have resulted from the 1933 book. Sister M. Corona Sharp took another look at the dramaturgical side of the play (*ShawR*, 1962), using the term *mask* to explain the ironic dialectic structure of the play—that "the catchwords and ambitions of each character are his or her individual mask; while the characters themselves are masks of human beings; and finally, the whole political game is a giant mask worn over the face of humanity." The "political game" that formed the living and shifting background of the play is described in S. Weintraub's *The Last Great Cause: The Intellectuals and the Spanish Civil War* (1968), where Shaw, during the period when the play was written, is shown as one of the "Aloof Olympians" of literature who claimed to stand above the battle. ("Spain must choose for itself; it is not really your business.")

In Good King Charles's Golden Days

Shaw's last prewar play was *In Good King Charles's Golden Days* (written 1938–39, revised 1946), which shifted his dramatizations of ways by which the world might be better governed backward in time to the period of Charles II. J. M. Keynes, in "G.B.S. and Isaac Newton" (in *G.B.S. 90*, ed. S. Winsten, 1946), observes that Shaw places the action of the play in 1680 and "with wild departure from the known facts he describes Newton as he certainly was not in that year. But with prophetic insight into the possibilities of his nature he gives us a picture which would not have been very unplausible thirty years later—*In Dull King George's Golden* (much more golden) *Days*." Another historical analysis worth examining is a twenty-page section of Roy's *Shaw's Historical Plays*, which examines the accuracy and imagination in a work that Shaw himself subtitled a "true history that never happened." N. O'Donnell (*ShawR*, 1958) suggests that the focus of the lengthy first-act discussion is the problem of knowledge and that what it reveals is "the possibility of a degree of harmony in the world of intellectual discussion which is ironically contrasted with the discord prevailing in the world of political action. . . ."

Extended studies of the later plays by Katherine Haynes Gatch and more recently by Hansrudolf Kamer will continue to be the basis for additional scrutiny of the last period of Shaw's playwriting; and to these may be added the several seminal studies of individual plays by F. P. W. McDowell. In "The Last Plays of Bernard Shaw: Dialectic and Despair" in *English Stage Comedy*, Gatch, having said earlier—in " 'The Real Sorrow of Great Men': Mr Bernard Shaw's Sense of Tragedy" (*CE*, 1947–48)—that the last plays have no obvious dramatic analogues, goes on to suggest that Shaw used "a dialectical structure from Hegel and Marx," modified by "the solvent of the comic spirit." In the later plays she sees a calculated ironic relationship between the magnitude of the themes and the triviality of the treatment, concluding that the plays are Shaw's response to a compulsion to find "new modes for our time." (It has been noted earlier that Huizinga saw a Hegelian approach to tragedy in *Saint Joan*; that Shaw's method generally resembles Hegelian synthetic dialectic is also one of Albert's observations in "Bernard Shaw: The Artist as Philosopher.") Kamer's *Künsterlische und politische Extravaganz im Spätwerk Shaws* (1973) examines the plays from *The Apple Cart* to *Farfetched Fables* as experiments in political and philosophical extravaganza, expressions of the interwar and immediate postwar years—disregarding realistic requirements and exploring new dramatic dimensions, including allegory and symbolic action.

Buoyant Billions and the Last Plays

Separate studies on Shaw's surprisingly sprightly first postwar play (begun 1936–37, re-begun in 1945, and completed when he was ninety in 1947) are few, the fullest of them McDowell's "The World, God, and World Bettering: Shaw's *Buoyant Billions*" (*BUSE*, 1957). "The continuity of Shaw's intellectual life" is demonstrated by the play, McDowell asserts. *Buoyant Billions* "should not be so much dismissed as a derivative work as studied for its apical significance in Shaw's development. Its forthright elaboration of long-held ideas and attitudes enables us, too, to glance backward and reinterpret the twentieth-century [Shavian] plays more surely in its mirrored image." Richard Nickson's "The World Betterer: Shav versus Shav" (*ShawR*, 1959) looks at the father-son conflict in the play as one between Shaw the pragmatist and Shaw the prophet. Several textual analyses by Steven Joyce, examining the BL typescript and rehearsal copies and rough proofs, illuminate the play, notably "The Ice Age Cometh: A Major Emendation of *Buoyant Billions* in Criticial Perspective," *SHAW* 7 (1987), the germ of a book-length study. Joyce's *Transformation and Texts: G. B. Shaw's "Buoyant Billions"* (1991) is a comprehensive examination of the manuscript and rehearsal copy stages, and of the changes made for the German premiere (in the Trebitsch translation), which, in 1948, was the first performance anywhere.

No useful separate or extended analyses of *Farfetched Fables* (written 1948) or the brief satirical puppet play *Shakes versus Shav* (written 1949) exist; but there is a study of Shaw's last play, *Why She Would Not* (written 1950). Dan H. Laurence's "The Facts about *Why She Would Not*" (*Theatre Arts*, August 1956) examines the shorthand manuscript numbered LIV in the canon by Shaw and defends its completeness, noting that the last page is dated "23/7/50 Ayot" and adds "End of Scene 5 and of the play."

10

Criticism in Languages Other Than English

The growing number of works on Shaw in languages other than English indicates a continuing interest that reaches beyond theatrical performance. The first significant book in the field, and still one of the most perceptive, is Julius Bab's *George Bernard Shaw*, published in Berlin in 1909 and updated in 1926. Few early foreign-language writers now need to be remembered, other than historically. One whose essays have only recently been translated is Lu Xun (Hsun), who wrote about Shaw in prewar China. In Florence Chien's "Lu Xun's Six Essays in Defense of Bernard Shaw," *SHAW* 12 (1992), five of the pieces appear in English for the first time.

A substantial list appears in part *K* of the Laurence *Bibliography*, from the *G. Bernard Shaw* of Gunnar Castren (1906), published in Finland, to Tatsuo Yamamoto's *Banado Sho* (1981), published in Tokyo. Some are general-purpose introductory studies meant to put Shaw in the perspective of the national culture, such as Anna Obraztsova's *Bernard Shou i evropeiskaia-teatralnaia kultura na rubezhe deviatnadtsatogo-dvadtsatogo veko*

(Moscow, 1974), Karl-Heinz Schoeps's *Bertolt Brecht und Bernard Shaw* (Bonn, 1974), Matahiko Ichikawa's *Warau Tetsujin Banado Sho* (Tokyo, 1975), and Asela Rodriguez-Seda de Laguna's *Shaw en el mundo hispánico* (Puerto Rico, 1981). Others concern themselves with specific aspects of Shaw, such as the sociolinguistic study by Ernst H. Andrecht, *Sprachsoziologische Aspekte in der dramatischen Sprachgestaltung Bernard Shaws* (Frankfurt, 1976). Jean-Claude Amalric's study, with extensive but superseded bibliographical apparatus, *Bernard Shaw: Du Reformateur victorien au prophete edouardien* (Paris, 1977), reveals its perspective in its title, as does Norbert Greiner's "Idealism *und* Realism *im Frühwerk George Bernard Shaws.*" Shaw's relationship to a French playwright of the thesis school is examined in Michel Pharand's "Iconoclasts of Social Reform: Eugene Brieux and Bernard Shaw" (*SHAW* 8, 1988), which also includes an essay by G. B. S. for the program of a 1913 London production of Brieux's *Woman on Her Own.* The impact of Shaw on Hermann Sudermann is analyzed in Walter T. Rix's "Shaw und Sudermann: Von der Gemeinsamkeit der Dramatiker und ihrer unerquicklichen Stücke beim Eintritt ins 20. Jahrhundert," in *Hermann Sudermann: Werk und Wirkung* (ed. W. T. Rix, Würzburg, 1980).

A collection of critical essays on Shaw has also appeared in Germany, *George Bernard Shaw,* edited by Kurt Otten and Gerd Rohmann (Darmstadt, 1978). Although the collection includes reprinted extracts in German from earlier German scholars, ranging from J. Bab (1909) and Johan Huizinga (1930) to F. Denninghaus (1971) and H. Kamer (1973), as well as extracts from familiar English-language pieces, it also includes others less familiar to English-language scholars. These are "Die religiose Bedeutung des Evolutionsgedankens bei Bernard Shaw" by Alfred Dutli (1950), "Sündenfall und übermensch in G. B. Shaws *Back to Methuselah*" by Rüdiger Reitemeier (1966), and "Shaws metabiologisches Testament in *Saint Joan*" by Gerd Rohmann 1976). The most recent Japanese scholarship in book form is *Research Essays on Bernard Shaw* by members of the Shaw Society of Japan (1986), in Japanese but with useful English abstracts. Coverage ranges from Shaw's Irish Protestant origins to the fantasy of his late plays.

11

Shaw in Fiction

An almost unmined area for research is Shaw's appearance in imaginative literature, a phenomenon far from uncommon among public figures who, from William Shakespeare to Sweeney Todd, have reached a status of near-myth. There has been little examination of where, and in what guise, Shaw appears as a fictional character in plays, short stories, poems, and novels not only by his contemporaries but in the years since. Such incarnations are not only indices of fame or notoriety but of how the individual is perceived at the time of writing.

Possibly the first such work limning Shaw was *The Paradox Club* (1886), a novel written at eighteen by the future editor and critic Edward Garnett. S. Weintraub furnishes the details in "The Garnetts, the Fabians and *The Paradox Club*," *ShawR* 2 (1957). Writing about the same era, Edith Nesbit Bland, whose pursuit of Shaw he had written about (almost certainly without her knowledge) in *An Unfinished Novel*, turned her view of the experience into a romantic novel, *Daphne in Fitzroy Street* (1909), described in Julia Briggs's *A Woman of Passion: The Life of E. Nesbit* (1987).

In editing J. M. Barrie's *Punch* for its first publication (*SHAW* 10, 1990—see below under Influence and Reputation), L. H. Hugo documents an Edwardian occasion in which Shaw appears as an onstage character. Other examples exist, but until R. F. Dietrich's "Shaw as Dramatic Icon" in *SHAW* 12 (1992) no attempt was made to collect dramatic examples. Many more remain to be located and identified, as not all of the fictional "Shaws" use his name.

Among the fantasy Shaws are those of Erica Cotterill, a cousin of Rupert Brooke's, who lusted for G.B.S. and pursued him to Ayot St. Lawrence. Her play *A Professional Socialist* (1908) and her novelized autobiography *An Account* (1916) are wildly passionate and badly written, but they evoke her unreciprocated feelings for Shaw. "Some Doctored Dilemma," by Robert Ross, and a 1908 novel by Ada Leverson, *Love's Shadow* (in a chapter, "Bruce's Play") are other Edwardian treatments of Shaw, both reprinted in *ShawR* 7 (1964).

From a self-mocking reference in *The Doctor's Dilemma* and a series of them in *Fanny's First Play,* to the young red-bearded Irishman who marries the Black Girl and the puppet co-star of *Shakes versus Shaw* drawn in his nineties, Shaw put himself in his writings. G.B.S.'s own self-portraits, overt and covert, repay investigation.

Writers continue to portray, parody, and poeticize Shaw beyond the grave, the most successful attempt commercially thus far being Jerome Kilty's *Dear Liar* (1960), a dramatization of the combative Shaw–Mrs. Patrick Campbell correspondence. Later plays exploited G.B.S. as a personality in one-man shows, Shaw's boyhood in Dublin, the high jinks surrounding the London opening of *Pygmalion*, and the Shaw–Dame Laurentia letters. The latter, Hugh Whitemore's *The Best of Friends* (1988), dramatizes the three-way correspondence that also includes Sydney Cockerell, beginning in 1924 and ending with Shaw's death.

There is even a subsection of writing about Shaw in which his plays and characters come to fictional life—Harry Johnston's sequel in novel form, *Mrs Warren's Daughter* (1920); the Chilean playwright Vincente Huidobro's *Gilles de Raiz* (1932), in which G.B.S. himself is a character; and, on the same theme, Michael Ayrton's "A Performance of *Saint Joan*" (1972), noted earlier under the play itself.

And the references to Shaw in fiction range the roster of twentieth-century novelists—H. G. Wells, Arnold Bennett, E. M. Forster, George Orwell, Anthony Burgess, Max Beerbohm, Henry Williamson, Laurence Durrell, David Lodge, "Saki" (H. H. Munro), and others. William Amos in *The Originals: An A–Z of Fiction's Real-Life Characters* (1985), ignores these yet suggests, surprisingly, Henry James's malign Peter Quint in *Turn of the Screw* (1898) and Professor George Edward Challenger in Arthur Conan Doyle's *The Lost World* (1912), *The Poison Belt* (1913), and *The Last of Mist* (1926).

Many minor authors have also used Shaw as a character. In a supporting role, Shaw appears in novels about Oscar Wilde and others of his contemporaries. But few writers have made Shaw the focus of a novel, as has Tullah Hanley in *The Strange Triangle of G.B.S.* (1956), which uses the novel form to portray the Shaw–Janet Achurch relationship without transgressing copyright legalities regarding their correspondence.

Edith Nesbit was very likely the first writer to use Shaw in fiction as well as verse. Among later writers, Ray Bradbury has also put him in both genres. His "G.B.S. and the Loin of Pork," satirizing Shaw's vegetarianism, is in *SHAW* 2 (1982) and collected in *The Complete Poems of Ray Bradbury* (1982). And Bradbury's science fiction "G.B.S.—Mark V," in *Long after Midnight* (1976), is a story in which Shaw materializes on a spaceship.

The range of Shavian representations in various imaginative literary forms suggests that further critical and biographical explorations are likely to repay the effort. More fictional Shaws are in print than are sampled here. Such Shaws are not only an index to reputation but a means of biographical and critical commentary that could not have been made in any other way in Shaw's lifetime. Myriad other inferences and possibilities for entertainment and elucidation can emerge from an examination of how writers creatively adapt real people to literary ends.

12

Influence and Reputation

The range and depth of Shaw's literary and extraliterary impact cannot be measured by influence studies, which remain insubstantial. In playwriting, the drama of his native Ireland has been profoundly—if reluctantly—affected; and although Sean O'Casey and Brendan Behan identified this aspect of their own work, the former (in his memoirs in particular) with profound reverence, the only comprehensive account is S. Weintraub's "Shaw's Other Keegan: O'Casey and G.B.S.," *Sean O'Casey Centenary Essays* (1980), ed. David Krause and R. R. Lowery, augmented in *Unexpected Shaw*. Shaw's stormy relationship with the Abbey Theatre is the only pertinent subject explored by other scholars. With respect to England the status of research into Shaw's influence is little better. The basic source is Desmond McCarthy's *The Court Theatre 1904–1907: A Commentary and Criticism* (1907), augmented in a 1966 edition by S. Weintraub with a transcript of the speeches by playwrights and critics at the testimonial dinner to John Vedrenne and Granville Barker on 7 July 1907, which includes Shaw's missionary address to potential writers for the stage. His attempts to entice major writers in other genres to write for the theater is well known, and his awkward involvement with James's theatrical ventures is told by Leon Edel in the fourth and fifth volumes of *Henry James*. There is a general survey, "The Edwardian Theatre and the Shadow of Shaw," by G. Weales in *Edwardians and Late Victorians*, ed. Richard Ellmann (1960), but Shaw's attempts, specifically, to lure Barrie, Conrad, Galsworthy, Moore, Wells, Bennett, Chesterton, and other contemporaries into playwriting are less well known, although Kinley E. Roby's "Arnold Bennett: Shaw's Ten O'Clock Scholar" (*ShawR*, 1970) examines one of the results and William B. Furlong's "Shaw and Chesterton: The Link was *Magic*" (*ShawR*, 1967) examines another.

While Barrie's domestic comedy *What Every Woman Knows* (1908) seems a remake of *Candida*, and *The Admirable Crichton* (1901) is a play of Shavian irony, the only study to make a connection is L. H. Hugo's "*Punch*: J. M. Barrie's Gentle Swipe at 'Supershaw' " (*SHAW* 10, 1990), which includes the first printing of the 1906 playlet. Shaw's impact on Galsworthy is demonstrated in James Gindin's "The Belated Shavian Influence: Wartime Disillusion and *The Foundations*," *SHAW* 10 (1990).

G.B.S.'s impact on the younger generation is inadequately researched. His close, two-way relationship with Granville Barker is analyzed by M. Morgan in her study of Barker, *A Drama of Political Man* (1961), and by Thomas Whitaker in "Granville Barker's Answer to *Heartbreak*" (*SHAW* 10, 1990); but, among Edwardians, no study of the Shavian impact on St. John Hankin, or even W. Somerset Maugham, appears to exist. One dramatist upon whom Shavian influence has been traced is W. B. Yeats, in S. Weintraub, "Uneasy Friendship: Shaw and Yeats," *Yeats* (1983). Striking literary influences upon another Irishman are probed in Weintraub's "A Respectful Distance: James Joyce and his Dublin Townsman Bernard Shaw" (*JML*, 1986), where *Ulysses* and *Finnegans Wake* are seen through a Shavian lens. Noel Coward confessed how much he owed to G.B.S. in his early work, especially to *You Never Can Tell*, in his memoir *Present*

Indicative (1937), but critics have not ranged beyond quoting Coward. James Bridie was known as the "Scottish G.B.S.," but again no extended criticism has evaluated the observation; and J. B. Priestley's own comments about his indebtedness to Shaw have evoked no corroborative studies. Among writers in the post–World War II generations several have been identified with Shaw for one reason or another, among them Nigel Dennis, John Whiting, and John Osborne, with Katherine J. Worth's article, "Shaw and John Osborne" (*Shavian*, 1964), and her book, *Revolutions in Modern English Drama* (1973), perhaps the best connections of Shaw with Osborne outside of Osborne himself, who has a character in *Epitaph for George Dillon* (1955) (the play he wrote with Anthony Creighton) tell Dillon, a playwright in the ranting Osborne mold, "Dialogue's not bad, but these great long speeches—that's a mistake. People want action, excitement. I know—you think you're Bernard Shaw. But where's he today? Eh? People won't listen to him."

Gabriele Scott Robinson's essay (*ShawR*, 1974) is the only close examination of relationships between Shaw and Whiting. B. F. Dukore's "*Red Noses* and *Saint Joan*" (*MD*, 1987), sees the Peter Barnes play as his response to *Joan* and concludes, "Despite the differences between the visions of these dramatists, the similarities of the two plays are strong."

Shavian influence has been identified in a number of European playwrights, notably Bertolt Brecht (whose own 1926 "Ovation for Shaw" made the fact of his Shavian interest clear), Friedrich Dürrenmatt, Max Frisch, Günter Grass, and Peter Weiss, among German-language playwrights; however, thorough explorations remain to be done. That Shaw's impact in European theater was both early and profound is evident not only from his having been widely translated and performed (Shaw even encouraged world premieres of several of his plays in Berlin, Vienna, and Warsaw) but from a thorough scrutiny of that early impact in J. J. Weisert's "Shaw in Central Europe before 1914" in *Anglo-German and American-German Crosscurrents* 2 (1962). (A worldwide scan of Shaw performances appears in

Lucile K. Henderson's "Shaw around the World" appendix to A. Henderson's *George Bernard Shaw: Man of the Century*, 1956.) Shavian influence in France, particularly in the impact of his *Saint Joan* on French historical drama, has been noted by D. C. Gerould (*ShawR*, 1964); while Judith S. Calvin (*ShawR*, 1962) analyzes the traces of Shavian thought and dramatic structure that "permeate" the works of Giraudoux. Curiously, this latter element has resulted in a forty-year time reversal in Maurice Valency's *The Cart and the Trumpet: The Plays of George Bernard Shaw*, where the critic—a translator of Giraudoux—observes of certain lines in *Major Barbara* that they "oddly recall the Ragpicker's wry speech in . . . *La Folle de Chaillot*." The Shavian impact upon Jean Anouilh has been profound but remains uninvestigated; nor do relationships between Shaw and Sartre appear to be usefully scrutinized, an exception being Ruby Cohn's "Hell on the Twentieth-Century Stage" (*WSCL*, 1964), which sees resemblances between *Don Juan in Hell* and *No Exit*, both pleasant "Palaces of Lies." In general, despite the lack of success of Shaw's plays (other than *Joan*) in France, his impact upon French playwrights has been substantial, although examined only superficially.

Shaw's influence in America largely remains to be explored in depth. S. Weintraub's "Bernard Shaw and the American Theatre," *UNISA English Studies* (South Africa, 1991), examines the impact of American plays on G.B.S. as well as his effect upon American playwrights, from David Belasco through Robert Sherwood, Eugene O'Neill, S. N. Behrman, Thornton Wilder, and into postwar theater. Zachary Bloomfield in "America's Response to George Bernard Shaw: A Study of Professional Productions, 1894–1905," *Theatre Studies* (1991), quotes usefully from contemporary critical reception in Shaw's first years on the American stage. Michael O'Hara deals with Shaw on the later American stage in "*On the Rocks* and the Federal Theatre Project" (*SHAW* 12, 1992), a subject briefly alluded to also in Weintraub.

Elmer Rice has discussed his own early interest in Shaw

(*ShawR*, 1957). Shaw's considerable impact on Eugene O'Neill is noted by Arthur and Barbara Gelb (*ShawR*, 1962, and in their biography, *O'Neill*, 1962); while Louis Shaeffer examines that impact more substantially, particularly in the second volume of his biography, *O'Neill: Son and Artist* (1973). S. N. Behrman, called by some the most notable American writer of high comedy, knew his Shaw and knew Shaw himself; but—except for some hints by Weales and Weintraub—no study of that relationship exists other than Behrman's own memories of Shaw in *The Suspended Drawing Room* (1965) and *People in a Diary* (1972). Perhaps the most substantial examination of Shavian influence upon an American playwright remains Anne N. Lausch's "Robert Sherwood's Heartbreak Houses" and "The Road to Rome by Way of Alexandria and Tavazzano" (*ShawR*, 1963). "The Time of His Life: A Shavian Influence," by D. Leary, in *William Saroyan: The Man and the Writer Remembered*, ed. Leo Hamalian (1987), sees strong Shavian echoes in Saroyan and quotes Saroyan himself to that effect.

Other playwrights of the 1930s and 1940s sought to invoke Shaw as a means of adding a dimension to their work, but there was little reciprocal praise from the crusty playwright. After sitting through a Clifford Odets screenplay, Shaw remarked that it was "inarticulate noises with American accents."

If one can accept T. S. Eliot, long resident in England, as American, at least one more play of the time can be pointed to as Shavian. When *Saint Joan* was produced, Eliot as editor of *The Criterion* (April 1926) disparaged it as "one of the most superstitious of the effigies which have been erected to that remarkable woman." It was a painful confession on his part, then, when he revealed in 1951 about the prose epilogue with the knightly tempters in *Murder in the Cathedral* (1935), "I may, for aught I know, have been slightly under the influence of *Saint Joan*. " It has since been suggested that the ritual chant of multiple voices at the close of the first act of *Heartbreak House* foreshadowed the choral technique employed by Eliot in *The Family Reunion* (1939), while his later, more accessible comedies employ wit and satire suggesting Wilde and Shaw. Eliot began his playwriting career, E. Bentley wrote in 1953, "in strong opposition to the drama in prose, drama of ideas, and drama by Bernard Shaw; *The Confidential Clerk* has all the earmarks of Shavianism as described by the early Eliot without the merits of the real Bernard Shaw. . . ."

The major American play of the World War II years, Thornton Wilder's *The Skin of Our Teeth* (1942), has been linked to James Joyce's *Finnegans Wake* as a burlesque history of mankind, yet a case can also be made for a Shavian dimension. *Back to Methuselah* had already inspired science fiction writers in drama and fiction from the Capek brothers to Olaf Stapledon; it was inevitable that what Shaw called his "metabiological pentateuch"—a history of the world from the Garden of Eden to the indefinable future—would make an impact in America. In Wilder's philosophical farce, dispensing with theatrical illusion at every turn, audiences discovered, as in Shaw's cycle, a Lilith (Sabina in *Skin of Our Teeth*) and a Cain (Henry in Wilder's play) who weave through time, and other elements suggesting that the playwright knew his Shaw as well as his Joyce, the elder dramatist attempting to find meaning during one world war, the younger writer seeking understanding during the next.

Postwar American dramatists largely turned to other sources of inspiration, although Tennessee Williams, who was at college in the 1930s, wrote a term paper on *Candida* and borrowed from *Heartbreak House* in the early play he wrote with Donald Windham, *You Touched Me!* (1942). The college essay is reproduced in *ShawR* (1977), while the *You Touched Me!* connection is explored by Weales in "Tennessee Williams Borrows a Little Shaw," *ShawR* (1965). That Williams kept reading Shaw is clear from his afterword to *Camino Real* (1953), in which he declared, "My own creed as a playwright is fairly close to that expressed by the painter in Shaw's play *The Doctor's Dilemma*: 'I believe in Michelangelo, Velasquez and Rembrandt; in the might of design, the mystery of color, the redemption of all things by beauty everlasting and the message of art that has made these hands blessed. Amen.' " And in the Expressionist qualities of the play itself, beyond time and space and containing figures like Don Quixote who are mythically embodied ideas, *Camino Real* echoes Shaw's own *Don Juan in Hell.*

An exception to the decline in Shavian influence was the musical theater, where *My Fair Lady* (1956), Alan Jay Lerner and Frederick Loewe's close adaptation of Shaw's *Pygmalion,* inaugurated a new era in the play-with-music in which song, dance, and lyrics arose out of situation and character. The revue musical with a thin book had been under attack by the integrated musical play since *Showboat* (1927), but that had proved an anomaly until *Oklahoma* in 1943. *My Fair Lady* brought the unified dramatic exeperience to the musical, in effect a new art form akin to opera but without its domination by the composer. In *My Fair Lady,* Lerner confided (*ShawR,* 1956), many of the lyrics and much of the dialogue came not only directly from *Pygmalion* but even from Shaw's preface.

Among postwar indebtednesses was Gore Vidal's historical satire *Romulus* (1962), with its open thefts from Shaw ("Thank heaven," says one character. "No, don't thank heaven, dear, thank me," quips Romulus, in a steal from Undershaft in *Major Barbara.*). And, although Edward Albee's *Who's Afraid of Virginia Woolf* (1963) has been equated with *Heartbreak House* as an unmasking game, with some lines uncannily parallel, little else in Albee is Shavian. Later playwrights have also gone elsewhere for inspiration, although plays in which wit coruscates and paradox abounds, like those of A. R. Gurney, are still often labeled Shavian. Of them, the most directly identifiable as in the G.B.S. vein is Richard Nelson's satirical *Some Americans Abroad* (1989), in which two characters discuss a London play they have seen. Philip waves it aside as "intellectual mush. . . . That's how Shaw works. . . . Shaw enjoyed trickiness, not real thinking." Joe, on the other hand, insists, "Come on, it was funny. You laughed. . . . I think that play is very profound." In several of his own plays, Shaw knocked down, tongue in cheek, his own work, and the process continues while playwrights simultaneously appropriate it.

Examination of Shaw's literary and stage impact, however preliminary, is further along than other, perhaps more essential, Shavian research. Political and social changes, accelerated even more in the twentieth century than heretofore, have accelerated changes in diction, idiom, and language in general, making Paul Kozelka's pioneering *A Glossary to the Plays of Bernard Shaw* (1959) the merest beginning. Variorum editions of the plays are thus one of the many needs in Shaw scholarship yet to be achieved. Much ephemeral writing remains in manuscript, particularly drafts of lectures; and these are likely to appear piecemeal rather than in any logical context. Many thousands of Shaw's extant letters remain unpublished because it was not economical for a commercial publisher to issue a selection of his correspondence in more than four volumes. The canon is likely both to increase and to become more accessible, the latter especially as Shavian copyrights (to work published by the time of his death) expire in Berne Convention countries.

Shaw's influence in areas not literary or theatrical has been extensive although seldom reevaluated since the events themselves. As an act of public statesmanship his pioneering battle for a National Theatre has been posthumously successful. He liked to think of himself as a municipal citizen, and his controversial public pronouncements on international affairs often show—with World War I very likely the exception—that he was more of a man of vision closer to home. In 1933, on his first American visit, he maintained to the mayor of San Francisco, "People think of me as a theatrical man, but I am really proud of having served six years as a municipal councillor." He had been awakened to civic issues by the same problems that evoked his early plays and wrote usefully on subjects such as municipal ownership of utilities (*The Common Sense of Municipal Trading* 1904), now widespread; he was also an effective local officeholder for the London borough of St. Pancras from 1897 to 1903, an experience surveyed by H. M. Geduld in "Bernard Shaw, Vestryman and Borough Councillor" in the now-defunct

California Shavian (1962) and—in shorter form—in *The Shavian* (1964). Shaw's contributions to national politics resulted initially from his leadership role in the Fabian Society, which led inevitably to the larger stage of the infant Labour Party. Both are extensively described in the autobiographical prefaces Shaw contributed to sixty years of succeeding editions of *Fabian Essays*, the first of which, in 1889, he edited.

Nothing more useful has yet appeared for evaluating Shaw's various extraliterary influences than *G.B.S. 90*, essays collected by S. Winsten to honor Shaw's ninetieth birthday. Included are J. B. Priestley on Shaw as social critic, J. D. Bernal on Shaw as scientist, Dean W. R. Inge on Shaw as theologian, Maurice Dobb on Shaw and economics, A. S. Neill on Shaw and education, Emil Davies on Shaw and local government, and Sir William Haley and Val Gielgud on Shaw and the growth of radio. There is little else by political or economic historians to isolate Shaw's genuine impact upon wage and hour legislation, municipalization of utilities and transportation, tax equalization, censorship, women's rights (but for *Fabian Feminist*), the National Health Acts, and other changes in the relationships between the people and their government.

The totality of Shaw's impact on the BBC in its formative years, the 1920s and 1930s, has yet to be examined. Some of his radio talks are printed in Laurence's *Platform and Pulpit*, and R. F. Bosworth's "Shaw Recordings at the BBC" (*ShawR*, 1964), suggests some of that influence. Vivian Ducat's "Bernard Shaw and the King's English" in *SHAW* 9, *Shaw Offstage* (1989) is a rare look at Shaw's influence as chairman of the BBC's Committee on Spoken English in the 1930s. (He would be appalled at the erosion since.)

Shaw's practical role in political affairs is very likely underestimated. A contemporary overview by various hands appears as *SHAW* 11, *Shaw and Politics* (T. F. Evans, 1991). S. Weintraub's *Journey to Heartbreak* demonstrates how seriously the government viewed him during the 1914–18 war and the reality of his impact—from gadfly to the architect of a real shift in opinion through his chairmanship of the Fabian Research Committee—in creating serious interest in international organization (and thus the postwar League of Nations). Perhaps his efforts to mold opinion about Ireland are also underestimated, for the Laurence and Greene edition of *The Matter with Ireland* shows that, however abortive and frustrated were Shaw's attempts to play a larger role than events permitted, he did help make Irish interests better known and more respectable. But his major public role may have been, in the longer view, on a smaller stage, although Emil Davies's wry forecast of a schoolgirl essay in the Shavian bicentenary year of 2056 deliberately exaggerates: "George Bernard Shaw was noted as an authority and pioneer in regard to municipal affairs. He was a London Borough Councillor and wrote a book entitled *The Common Sense of Municipal Trading* which has become a classic. He also wrote some plays."

Shaw's significance, even at the height of his fame, was suspect to some of the most acute minds among his contemporaries. "Have you seen any more of your friends who worship Bernard Shaw?" George Orwell asked Brenda Salkeld (ca. 10 March 1933). "Tell them that Shaw is Carlyle & water, that he ought to have been a Quaker (cocoa and commercial dishonesty), that he has squandered whatever talents he may have had back in the '80s in inventing metaphysical reasons for behaving like a scoundrel, that he suffers from an inferiority complex towards Shakespeare, & that he is the critic . . . that Samuel Butler prayed to be delivered from. Say that Shaw's best work was one or two early novels & one or two criticisms he wrote for the *Saturday Review* when Harris was editor, & that since then it has got steadily worse until its only function is to console fat women who yearn to be highbrows."

That the adjective *Shavian* has gone into the language, and appears in all major dictionaries, is a clue not only to the extent of Shaw's influence but to the solidity of his reputation. Retiring as theater critic for the *Saturday Review* in 1898, just after he had begun *Caesar and Cleopatra*, Shaw in his forty-second year (and bedridden with a serious foot infection) joked in a valedictory column, "I may dodder and I may dote; I may potboil and platitudinize; I may become the butt and chopping-block of all the bright, original spirits of the rising generation; but my reputation shall not suffer: it is built up fast and solid, like Shakespeare's, on an impregnable basis of dogmatic reiteration." A half-century later Shakespeare remained to him the supreme dramatic poet, however unoriginal the ideas or the ethics he dramatized; and in the puppet play *Shakes versus Shav* (1949) the ninety-four-year-old Shaw's alter ego appeals to "Shakes,"

> Peace, jealous Bard.
> We are both mortal. For a moment to suffer
> My glimmering light to shine.

The comparison continues to be made. Although each master used the stage in his own way, each was without peer as creator of a lasting canon. J.I.M. Stewart in the twentieth-century volume of the *Oxford History of English Literature (Eight Modern Writers)* invokes the Bard in calling *Saint Joan* "conceivably the finest and most moving English drama since *The Winter's Tale* or *The Tempest*." Gore Vidal in *Homage to Daniel Shays* sought the same figure of speech in writing, "I should put quite plainly here at the beginning that I regard Bernard Shaw as the best and most useful dramatist in English since the author of *Much Ado about Nothing* turned gentleman and let fall the feather."

Among brief general evaluations, the bleakest is Angus Wilson's centenary "The Living Dead—IV: Bernard Shaw" (*LonM*, 1956); like Alexander Woolcott in 1920, who felt that the very elements which endowed Shaw's work with "Force and value and significance" could doom it "to grow stale like the headlines of yesteryear," Wilson saw the plays as battles in the trenches of the last war. Seeing beyond the journalistic dimension is F.P.W. McDowell's "Another Look at Bernard Shaw: A Reassessment of His Dramatic Theory, His Practice and His Achievement" (*DramaS*, 1961), which examines the dramatic tension the playwright secures between realism and artifice, his "sensitivity to the manifold resources of language," and the vigorous life given to large ideas—the "fusion of comic inventiveness with probing intelligence" in the service of "ethical idealism." But some serious critics continue to cavil at the kind of life given to particular Shavian ideas. According to Allardyce Nicoll in *English Drama 1900–1930: The Beginnings of the Modern Period* (1973), Shaw was an incautious in his thinking as he was brilliant and scintillating and "apt to seize upon conclusions without considering their implications, inclined to lose sight of humanity in the process of ratiocination. . . . Fortunately, however, Shaw's rather jejune but dangerous personal philosophizings were accompanied by other qualities, and especially by his effervescent sense of fun, by his innate theatrical skill and, perhaps most important of all, by his idiosyncratic treatment of his stage figures." On balance, nevertheless, G.B.S. remains to Nicoll "this dramatic colossus," an epithet inapplicable in his terms to any other figure in English drama since 1616. With less hesitation an anonymous critic in *TLS* (24 May 1974) observed that "Shaw can combine psychological generosity with merciless social analysis (not to mention exhilarating theatricality). . . . Shaw seems old fashioned [only] because he allows both sides their most persuasive arguments and their human dignity."

Perhaps the chairman of the Nobel Committee of the Swedish Academy, Per Hallström, summed up Shaw as well in his lifetime as has been done since in awarding him the prize for literature (1925), finding "beneath all his sportiveness and defiance . . . both idealism and humanity, [his] stimulating satire often being infused with a singular poetic beauty." Combining caution with encomium he added that although Shaw's "criticism of society and his perspective of its course of development may have appeared too nakedly logical, too hastily thought out, too unorganically simplified. . . . His struggle against traditional conceptions that rest on no solid basis and against traditional feelings that are either spurious or only half genuine, has borne witness to the loftiness of his aims."

In "Shaw and the Passionate Mind" in Eric Salmon's *Is the Theatre Still Dying?* (1985), Shaw's value remains better seen in theatrical terms. "It is not true," says Salmon, "that the Shavian sense of the world translates everything into intellectual terms, nor is the intellect substituted for all other functions and activities, but that part of human perception which is naturally and normally made up of intellectual qualities is reflected, examined and illuminated by these plays: and the catching of the intellectual part of human experience at the very moment of crisis, tension and division was the aesthetic impulse that excited Shaw and made him into a dramatist. About that intellectual crisis . . . he was passionate."

Although Shaw's influence on the present generation of playwrights is receding, if one judges by their remarks or by contemporary studies of their works, the evidence is that he maintains his status as a twentieth-century master and remains much published, much examined and reexamined, and much read. Further, biographical evidence emerging from studies of his contemporaries and immediate successors confirms that his influence among his peers was profound. The many productions of his plays, even a television dramatization of an 1881 novel that sank almost without trace on first publication, suggest the intrinsic liveliness of his work—as he put it, the jam that made the pill go down.

The pill itself will remain a problem in accessibility for some of Shaw's plays and much of his prose. The Marxist element in the Shavian phamacopoeia had lost its credibility even as Shaw continued to ignore the persuasive, and pervasive, evidence that Stalinism had debased the ideal. And the ideal itself has now collapsed under strains that even Shaw had recognized from the start it could not bear. How his work generated by that dream survives shorn of its Marxist dimension will be a challenge to readers, audiences, scholars, directors, and actors. Does its philosophical core remain valid in practical human terms? Is the dramatic action any less cogent? Is the satire any less biting? Do the tensions that enliven a *Mrs Warren's Profession* or a *Major*

Barbara fail to survive their contemporaneity? Are they diminished as they are played, or visualized, in "period"? Is the wit of *The Apple Cart* lost with its futurism, the play having been set in a yet-to-be 1960? Is *The Millionairess* the victim of its implicit attack upon a rapacious Capitalism or a *Man and Superman* rendered obsolete by the omnipresence of the automobile? Did his Carlylean love affair with authoritarian figures turn some of his plays into yesterday's newspaper?

Even the ubiquitous Shavian fun may still inhibit understanding of his work. As Robert Whitman put it in *Shaw and the Play of Ideas* (1977), Shaw "embodied his ideas in such delightfully witty essays and plays that there has been a very real danger . . . that the wisdom would get lost in the fun. . . . Shaw as thinker has, for both critics and readers, had to play a somewhat sour second fiddle to Shaw the comic draftsman, Shaw the pre-absurdist, Shaw the post-Victorian, and of course Shaw the writer of musical comedy." While Shaw the thinker is indeed taken seriously, the other Shaws that were facets of his life and work continue to exercise greater fascination. The self-described "pantomime ostrich" discovered in life that the animal, once invented, was difficult to conceal.

Oscar Wilde once joked that while he had put his talent into his writings, he had put his genius into his life. Shaw would not have underplayed his own art, although on occasion he would claim that he was primarily a journalist in order to emphasize the here-and-now in his work. Yet much of it has now survived its time and place into other dimensions of significance—the reason, thus, for these pages.

13

A Guide to Acronyms and Abbreviations

BRH	*Bulletin of Research in the Humanities*
BUSE	*Boston University Studies in English*
CD	*Child Development*
CE	*College English*
CL	*Comparative Literature*
CLQ	*Colby Library Quarterly*
CVE	*Cahiers Victoriens et Edouardiens: Revue du Centre d'Etudes et de Recherches Victoriennes et Edouardiennes de l'Université Paul Valéry, Montpellier*
DAI	*Dissertation Abstracts International*
DramaS	*Drama Survey*
Eire	*Eire-Ireland: A Journal of Irish Studies* (St. Paul, Minn.)
ELH	*Journal of English Literary History*
ELN	*English Language Notes* (University of Colorado)
ELT	*English Literature in Transition (1880–1920)*
EngS	*Englische Studien*
ES	*English Studies*
ESC	*English Studies in Canada*
ETJ	*Educational Theatre Journal*
FortR	*Fortnightly Review*
IUR	*Irish University Review*

JAAC	*Journal of Aesthetics and Art Criticism*
JEGP	*Journal of English and Germanic Philology*
JJQ	*James Joyce Quarterly* (University of Tulsa)
JML	*Journal of Modern Literature*
KR	*Kenyon Review*
LCUT	*Library Chronicle of the University of Texas*
LonM	*London Magazine*
MD	*Modern Drama*
MLQ	*Modern Language Quarterly*
NewS	*New Statesman*
PMLA	*Publications of the Modern Language Association of America*
PQ	*Philological Quarterly* (Iowa City)
PsyR	*Psychoanalytic Review*
QJS	*Quarterly Journal of Speech*
QQ	*Queen's Quarterly*
RLV	*Revue des Langues Vivantes* (Brussels)
SAQ	*South Atlantic Quarterly*
SHAW	*SHAW: The Annual of Bernard Shaw Studies*
ShawR	*Shaw Review*
SJW	*Shakespeare-Jahrbuch* (Weimar)
SQ	*Shakespeare Quarterly*
TA	*Theatre Annual*
TCL	*Twentieth-Century Literature*
TDR	*The Drama Review* (formerly *Tulane Drama Review*)
ThS	*Theatre Survey* (American Society for Theatre Research)
TLS	*[London] Times Literary Supplement*
TSLL	*Texas Studies in Literature and Language*
UTQ	*University of Toronto Quarterly*
VP	*Victorian Poetry* (Morgantown, W.Va.)
VS	*Victorian Studies* (Indiana University)
WascanaR	*Wascana Review*
WSCL	*Wisconsin Studies in Comparative Literature*
YES	*Yearbook of English Studies*

Index of Authors

Abbott, Anthony S., 45, 87, 88
Adams, Elsie B., 8, 28, 42, 43, 66, 84
Albert, Sidney P., 28, 32, 43, 50, 79–80, 119
Albrecht, Michael von, 79, 108
Altman, Ross, 107
Altrincham, Lord, 109
Amalric, Jean-Claude, 28, 76, 122
Amos, William, 29, 126
Andrecht, Ernst H., 122
Aquino, John, 100
Armstrong, W. A., 50
Auden, W. H., 49
Ayrton, Michael, 103, 126

Bab, Julius, 121, 122
Baker, Stuart E., 82
Barber, George S., 56
Barnet, Sylvan, 104
Barr, Alan P., 45, 58, 87
Barrick, Mac E., 74
Barzun, Jacques, 29, 49
Baskin, Ken A., 82
Bax, Clifford, 15
Beardsmore, Hugo, 93
Beerbohm, Max, 47, 81–82
Behrman, S. N., 132
Bentley, Eric, 37, 63, 66, 74, 85, 92, 109, 133
Bentley, Joseph, 75
Bergquist, Gordon N., 59
Bermel, Albert, 77, 103
Bernal, J. D., 136
Berst, Charles A., 3, 15, 26, 28, 38, 40, 52, 61, 64, 65, 66–67, 68, 72, 73, 76, 81, 87, 92, 93, 98, 109
Bertin, Michael, 29
Bertolini, John A., 42, 69, 83, 106
Bevan, E. Dean, 10
Bissell, Claude, 52
Bitonti, Tracy Simmons, 63–64
Blanch, R. J., 75
Bland, Edith Nesbit, 124, 126
Blissett, William, 58
Bloom, Harold, 46
Bloomfield, Zachary, 131
Boas, Frederick S., 104
Bonham-Carter, Victor, 31
Bosch, Marianne, 115
Bosworth, R. F., 136

Bowman, David H., 76, 80–81
Boxill, Roger, 84
Bradbury, Ray, 126
Briden, E. F., 94
Briggs, Julia, 31, 125
Bringle, Jerald E., 11, 54, 55, 61
Britain, I. M., 18
Brophy, Brigid, 27
Bullough, Geoffrey, 64
Burton, Richard, 35

Calvin, Judith S., 131
Carpenter, Charles A., Jr., 38, 40, 61, 62, 77, 89
Carr, Pat M., 41
Cash, William P., 22
Castren, Gunnar, 121
Cavanaugh, Hilayne, 13
Chappelow, Allen, 24
Chesterton, G. K., 34
Chien, Florence, 121
Churchill, Winston, 36
Clurman, Harold, 98
Cockerell, Sydney C., 23
Cohen, M. A., 106
Cohn, Ruby, 131
Coleman, D. C., 98
Corballis, Richard, 56
Corrigan, D. Felicitas, 15
Corrigan, Robert, 95
Coskren, Robert, 40, 56, 58
Costello, Donald P., 10, 50, 92
Cotterill, Erica, 125
Couchman, Gordon W., 71, 72
Coxe, Louis, 69–70
Crawford, Fred D., 3, 54, 101
Creel, James Melton, 91
Crompton, Louis, 13, 38–39, 65, 66, 69, 71, 76, 79, 80, 83, 92–93, 96, 101, 103

Davies, Emil, 136, 137
Davies, Robertson, 75
Deans, Marjorie, 10, 24
Delacorte, Valerie Pascal, 24
Denninghaus, Friedhelm, 116, 122
Dent, Alan, 15
Dervin, Daniel, 32
Dietrich, R. F., 52, 125
Dobb, Maurice, 136
Dolid, William A., 64
Donahy, Henry J., 108
Downer, Alan J., 85
DuCann, C. G. L., 26
Ducat, Vivian, 136
Duerksen, Roland, 73
Dukore, Bernard F., 3, 10, 11, 13, 16, 28, 39, 45, 50, 61, 79, 81, 82, 86, 89, 90, 91, 92, 105, 110, 114, 115, 130
Dunbar, Janet, 25
Dunlap, Joseph R., 31
Dutli, Alfred, 122

Edel, Leon, 129
Eliot, T. S., 102, 132–33
Elliot, Vivian, 15
Erikson, Erik H., 32
Ervine, St. John, 23
Evans, T. F., 28, 30, 102, 136
Everding, Robert, 86, 111

Farmer, Henry George, 25
Farr, Diana, 31
Fergusson, Francis, 81
Ferrar, Harold, 78
Fielden, John, 103–4
Finney, Gail, 66
Fisher, Barbara, 89
Fiske, Irving, 68, 96
Forster, E. M., 62
Foster, Richard, 101
Frank, Joseph W., 80, 99, 101
Frankel, Charles, 81
Furlong, William B., 27, 129

Ganz, Arthur, 40, 42, 58
Garnett, Edward, 124
Gassner, John, 48, 58
Gatch, Katherine Haynes, 114, 118–19
Geduld, Harry M., 13, 61, 99–100, 135
Gelb, Arthur, 132
Gelb, Barbara, 132
Gerould, Daniel C., 57–58, 102, 131

Gibbs, A. M., 28, 42
Gielgud, Val, 136
Gill, Richard, 97
Gindin, James, 129
Goldberg, Michael, 94
Goodman, Phyllis, 53
Gordon, David J., 47
Gray, Piers, 28
Grecco, Stephen R., 64
Green, Benny, 30–31
Greene, David H., 12, 59
Greer, Germaine, 42–43
Greiner, Norbert, 68, 122
Grene, Nicholas, 15, 28, 42, 52
Griffin, Alice, 102

Haberman, Donald C., 8
Haley, William, 136
Hamon, Augustin, 34
Hanley, Tullah, 26, 126
Hardwick, Michael, 41
Hardwick, Mollie, 41
Hark, Ina Rae, 74, 90
Harris, Frank, 21, 22
Harris, Nathaniel, 29
Hartnoll, Phyllis, 41
Henderson, Archibald, 21–22, 95, 131
Henderson, Lucile Kelling, 42, 131
Hendrick, George, 31
Henson, Janice, 58
Herr, Linda, 70
Higgs, Calvin T., Jr., 65
Hill, Eldon C., 41
Hill, Holly, 107
Hogan, Robert, 12, 52, 53, 90
Holland, Michael J., 54
Holmes, Maurice, 52
Holroyd, Michael, 20, 27, 44, 46, 50
Holt, Charles Loyd, 56, 67
Howe, Percival P., 35
Hubenka, Lloyd, 13
Huggett, Richard, 94
Hugo, Betty, 26
Hugo, Leon H., 3, 28, 39, 54, 125, 129
Huidobro, Vincente, 126
Huizinga, Johan, 103, 119, 122
Hummert, Paul A., 43, 111, 114–15
Hyde, Mary, 15

Ichikawa, Matahiko, 122
Inge, Dean W. R., 136
Irvine, William, 22, 23, 37, 98, 106

Jackson, Holbrook, 33
Jay, Bill, 13
Jenckes, Norma, 11
Joad, C. E. M., 12, 44, 45
Johnson, Betty Freeman, 64
Johnson, Josephine, 15
Johnston, Harry, 126
Joyce, Steven, 120

Kalmar, Jack, 57
Kalogjera, Damir, 28
Kamer, Hansrudolf, 118, 119, 122
Kan, J. van, 103
Kapp, Yvonne, 31
Kaufman, Michael W., 98
Kaufmann, R. J., 46, 68
Kaul, A. N., 106
Kaye, Julian B., 37, 43, 80, 96, 97
Kennedy, Andrew, 46
Keunen, J., 68
Keynes, J. M., 118
Kiernan, Ryan, 53
Kilty, Jerome, 125
Klaus, H. Gustav, 53
Knepper, B. G., 63, 100
Kosok, Heinz, 78
Kozelka, Paul, 135
Krause, David, 29
Kronenberger, Louis, 46, 49, 76
Krutch, Joseph Wood, 47, 112

Laden, Alice, 27
Laguna, Asela Rodriguez-Seda de, 122
Langner, Lawrence, 23–24, 100, 104, 117
Larson, Gale K., 71
Laurence, Dan H., 3, 6, 7, 10, 12, 13–14, 15, 16–17, 19, 25, 27–28, 30, 56, 59, 88, 101, 120, 121, 136
Lausch, Anne N., 132

Leary, Daniel J., 10, 11, 13–14, 41, 45, 50, 72–73, 77, 96, 101, 110, 113, 115, 132
Lee, Josephine, 56
Lerner, Alan Jay, 91, 134
Leverson, Ada, 125
Lindblad, Ishrat, 28, 40, 61
Loewenstein, F. E., 52
Lorichs, Sonja, 43
Lowery, R. R., 29
Lu Xun (Hsun), 121
Ludeke, H., 72
Lutz, Jerry, 116

MacCarthy, Desmond, 33–34, 47, 81, 87, 105, 128
MacKenzie, Jeanne, 31–32
MacKenzie, Norman, 31–32
Macksoud, S. John, 107
Mandel, Oscar, 75
Mander, Raymond, 38
Martin, Murray, 28, 113
Martz, Louis, 104, 106
Matlaw, Myron, 90, 91
Matoba, Junko, 28
Matual, David, 88
Maude, Cyril, 21
May, Keith, 18, 58
Mayne, Fred, 46, 93
McCabe, Joseph, 34
McCarthy, Mary, 97
McDowell, Frederick P. W., 3, 17, 70, 76, 78, 86, 97–98, 102, 109, 110, 111, 112–13, 118, 119, 138–39
McKee, Irving, 102
McMillin, Scott, 110
Meisel, Martin, 37, 67, 68, 72, 78, 84, 87, 88
Mencken, H. L., 33, 47
Mendelsohn, Michael J., 95
Meyers, Jeffrey, 31
Mills, Carl Henry, 75–76
Mills, John A., 46, 93
Minney, R. J., 23, 27
Mitchell, Breon, 15
Mitchenson, Joe, 38
Mizener, Arthur, 106
Moore, Margaret, 13
Moore, Mavor, 29
Morgan, Margery, 11, 39, 41, 63, 76, 78, 80, 83–84, 85, 86, 98, 101, 108, 112, 113, 114, 117, 129
Morrow, Sean, 54
Mosley, Oswald, 58

Nathan, George Jean, 47
Neill, A. S., 136
Nelson, Raymond S., 68, 78, 87, 88, 89, 113
Nesbit, Edith (*see* Bland, Edith Nesbit)
Nethercot, Arthur H., 26–27, 32, 38, 66, 95
Nichols, Marie Hochmuth, 30
Nickson, Richard, 119–20
Nicoll, Allardyce, 139
Norwood, Gilbert, 79
Novick, Julius, 11, 62

O'Bolger, T. D., 21
O'Casey, Eileen, 24
O'Connor, Mary, 29
O'Donnell, Norbert F., 83, 110, 118
O'Donovan, John, 25, 27, 41–42
O'Driscoll, Robert, 78
O'Hara, Michael, 131
Obraztsova, Anna, 107, 121
Ohmann, Richard, 46, 77
Otten, Kurt, 122
Owens, Harold, 35

Palmer, John, 35
Parsons, Melinda Boyd, 57
Patch, Blanche, 19, 23
Pearson, Hesketh, 21, 22
Peart, Barbara, 66
Peters, Margot, 11, 27, 28, 109, 114
Peters (Vogt), Sally, 89, 116
Pfeiffer, John R., 3, 8, 100
Pharand, Michel, 44–45, 122
Pierson, Stanley, 30
Pilecki, G. A., 117
Pirandello, Luigi, 105
Pollak, Paulina Salz, 56
Porter, Stephen, 50
Priestley, J. B., 136

Purdom, C. B., 15, 27, 32
Putzell, Sara Moore, 94

Quinn, Martin, 16–17, 82, 98–99

Rabey, David I., 30, 110–11
Rambeau, James, 16
Rao, E. Nageswara, 52, 54
Rao, Valli, 28, 64, 101, 113
Rattray, R. F., 23
Redmond, James, 75, 108
Reinert, Otto, 71–72
Reitemeier, Rüdiger, 122
Rice, Elmer, 131
Richardson, Henry B., 93
Richter, H., 34
Riddle, Carol, 69
Rider, Dan J., 51
Rix, Walter T., 122
Robertson, John Mackinnon, 102
Robinson, Gabriele Scott, 130
Roby, Kinley E., 61, 129
Rodenbeck, John, 52, 116
Rohmann, Gerd, 122
Roll-Hansen, Diderik, 62
Rosen, Charles, 56
Rosenberg, Edgar, 16
Rosenblood, Norman, 55
Ross, Julian, 45
Ross, Robert, 125
Rosset, B. C., 25, 56, 85–86, 90
Roy, R. N., 43–44, 67, 118
Royall, Walter L., 68
Rudman, Harry W., 105
Rumball, Louise, 24
Russell, Annie, 30
Rypins, Stanley, 19

Salmon, Eric, 15, 27, 32, 140
Sarolea, Charles, 102
Saxe, Joseph, 93
Schoeps, Karl-Heinz, 122
Scott, Dixon, 34–35, 45
Scully, Frank, 21
Searle, William, 103, 106
Sen Gupta, S. C., 44
Shaeffer, Louis, 132
Sharp, Sister M. Corona, 117
Sharp, William, 85
Shattuck, Charles, 61
Shaw, Charles Macmahon, 29
Sidhu, C. D., 39
Sidnell, M. J., 78
Silver, Arnold, 29, 93, 109
Silverman, Albert H., 114
Silverstein, Paul, 90
Skidelsky, Robert, 27
Small, Barbara, 40
Smith, J. Percy, 11, 26, 71, 82, 83
Smith, Warren S., 12, 13, 45, 61, 77, 87, 101, 108
Smoker, Barbara, 27
Solomon, Stanley J., 85, 92, 104
Speckhard, Robert R., 117
Sprigg, Christopher St. John (Christopher Caudwell), 48
St. John, Christopher, 15
Stamm, Rudolph, 115
Stanbrook, Nuns of, 15
Stanton, Stephen, 63, 65
Stewart, J. I. M., 41, 106, 138
Stockholder, Fred E., 99
Stokes, E. E., 110
Stone (-Blackburn), Susan C., 87, 117
Stoppel, Hans, 103
Strauss, Erich, 48, 59
Sutton, Graham, 35

Tahir, Laura, 44
Tauber, Abraham, 46
Tippett, Michael, 100
Tompkins, Peter, 15, 26
Turco, Alfred, Jr., 18, 41, 44, 63, 83
Tyson, Brian F., 13, 62, 63, 104

Ussher, Arland, 38, 107

Valency, Maurice, 39, 74, 76, 87, 88, 89, 131
Veilleux, Jere Shanor, 78
Vesonder, Timothy, 40, 73, 94
Vidal, Gore, 96, 134, 138

Walker, John, 73
Wall, Vincent, 26
Wasserman, Marlie P., 64

Watson, Barbara B., 32, 43, 81
Weales, Gerald, 45, 57, 87, 106, 129, 131, 132, 133
Wearing, J. P., 7
Weimer, Michael, 90
Weintraub, Rodelle, 11, 15, 28, 32, 41, 42, 55, 61, 69, 74, 86–87
Weintraub, Stanley, 11, 13, 14, 15, 16, 19, 20, 25, 27, 28, 29, 31, 35, 50, 51, 52, 53, 54, 55, 57, 59, 66, 69, 71, 72, 74, 80, 83, 84, 89, 90–91, 94, 95, 96, 97, 101, 104, 107, 108, 109–10, 111, 114, 117–18, 124, 128, 129, 131, 132, 136
Weisert, John J., 28, 116, 130
Weiss, Samuel, 15, 65
Weissman, Philip, 32, 93
Wellwarth, George E., 64, 108
Werner, Jack, 14
West, Alick, 48, 107
West, E. J., 12, 15, 102, 115
Whitaker, Thomas R., 99, 129
Whitemore, Hugh, 125
Whiting, George W., 72
Whitman, Robert F., 11, 44, 69, 141
Williamson, Audrey, 23
Wilson, Angus, 138
Wilson, Colin, 39, 45, 96
Wilson, Edmund, 47, 49, 77, 105, 109
Wilson, Edwin, 116
Winsten, Stephen, 23, 44, 46, 118, 136
Wisenthal, J. L., 11, 17, 38, 43, 58, 73, 76, 78, 81, 115–16
Woodbridge, Homer, 39
Woodfield, James, 99
Worth, Katherine J., 130
Wright, Anne, 11, 94–96, 99

Yamamoto, Tatsuo, 121
Yorks, Samuel A., 45
Young, Stark, 97

Index of Works

"A.D. 3,000. The True Report of a County Councillor's Dream," 54
Admirable Bashville, The, 89
Adventures of the Black Girl in Search of God, The, 13, 53, 54
Advice to a Young Critic [R. Golding Bright) *and Other Letters*, 15
"Aerial Football," 55
Agitations: Letters to the Press, 16
Androcles and the Lion, 50, 87
Annajanska; or The Bolshevik Empress, 91
Apple Cart, The, 41, 64, 108–9, 112, 119, 141
Arms and the Man, 10, 11, 13, 65, 73
Ayot St. Lawrence Edition (*Collected Edition*), 12, 52, 55, 59

Back to Methuselah, 25, 35, 38, 61, 74, 76, 99–102, 108, 122, 133
"Ballads by Shaw: The Anonymous *Star* Versifier of 1888–89," 14
Bernard Shaw and Alfred Douglas: A Correspondence, 15
Bernard Shaw and Mrs. Patrick Campbell: Their Correspondence, 15
"Bernard Shaw at Oxford: GBS's Lecture on Playwriting," 11
Bernard Shaw, Early Texts: Play Manuscripts in Facsimile, 10
Bernard Shaw, Lady Gregory, and the Abbey, 15
Bernard Shaw on Language, 46
Bernard Shaw on the London Art Scene, 1885–1950, 16, 57
Bernard Shaw: Practical Politics, 13
Bernard Shaw's Arms and the Man: *A Composite Production Book*, 13
Bernard Shaw's Book Reviews Originally Published in the Pall Mall Gazette from 1885 to 1888, 13
Bernard Shaw's Letters to Granville Barker, 15, 32
Bernard Shaw's Letters to Siegfried Trebitsch, 15
Bernard Shaw's Nondramatic Literary Criticism, 13, 57
"Bernard Shaw's Works of Fiction: Reviewed by Himself," 51

Bernard Shaw: The Diaries 1885–1897, with early autobiographical notebooks and diaries, and an abortive 1917 diary, 19, 20, 30, 31, 51, 52, 66
Bodley Head Edition of Collected Plays and Their Prefaces, 9, 75, 112
Buoyant Billions, 119–20

Caesar and Cleopatra, 10, 11, 40, 50, 71–73, 137
Candida, 11, 29, 38, 40, 43, 60, 64, 65–67, 90, 129, 133
Captain Brassbound's Conversion, 11, 73–74
Cashel Byron's Profession, 51, 53, 89, 114
Cassone, The, 9
Collected Letters of Bernad Shaw, 14, 15, 16
Collected Screenplays, 50
Common Sense About the War, 35
Common Sense of Municipal Trading, The, 135, 137
Complete Prefaces, 10
Concordance to the Plays and Prefaces of Bernard Shaw, 10
Crude Criminology, 12
Cymbeline Refinished, 115–16

Dark Lady of the Sonnets, 13, 89, 116
Dear Mr. Shaw, 15
Devil's Disciple, The, 10, 11, 68–69, 83, 96
Doctors' Delusions, 12
Doctor's Dilemma, The, 11, 31, 69, 82–84, 125, 133
"Don Giovanni Explains," 55, 75, 76
Don Juan in Hell, 55, 75, 76, 131
Drama Observed, The, 16

"Early GBS Love Poem, An," 14
Ellen Terry and Bernard Shaw: A Correspondence, 15
"Emperor and the Little Girl, The," 54, 55
Essays in Fabian Socialism, 12

Fabian Essays, 12, 136
Fanny's First Play, 31, 41, 85, 88–89, 125
Farfetched Fables, 119, 120
Fascinating Founding, The, 90
"Fiction and Truth," 57
Florence Farr, Bernard Shaw, W. B. Yeats: Letters, 15
Flyleaves, 13
"From Dickens to Ibsen," 17
"From the Housetops," 14

Garden of the Hesperides, The, 9
G. Bernard Shaw 1856–1950: Photographer and Critic, 13, 57
Geneva, 108, 116–18
Getting Married, 62, 64, 84–85
Gospel of the Brothers Barnabas, 108

Haymarket Theatre: Some Records and Reminiscences, The (Chapter XXVII), 21
Heartbreak House, 10, 11, 17, 25, 32, 35, 44, 64, 73, 94–99, 100, 101, 111, 132, 133, 134
The Household of Joseph, 61
"How Frank Would Have Done It," 21
How He Lied to Her Husband, 11, 50, 90
How to Become a Musical Critic, 12, 56

Immaturity, 11, 20, 21, 32, 51, 52
In a Great Tradition: Tribute to Dame Laurentia McLachlan, Abbess of Stanbrook, 15
In Good King Charles's Golden Days, 41, 118–19
Interlude at the Playhouse, The, 90
Irrational Knot, The, 52

Jitta's Atonement, 90–91
John Bull's Other Island, 41, 64, 77–79

"Lecture on Shakespeare's *Troilus and Cressida*," 13
Letters from George Bernard Shaw to Miss Alma Murray (Mrs. Alfred Foreman), 14

London Music in 1888–89, 20, 32
Love among the Artists, 11, 51, 53

Major Barbara, 10, 11, 24, 30, 33, 34, 40, 41, 44, 50, 58, 61–62, 64, 73, 79–82, 98, 108, 131, 134, 140
Man and Superman, 29, 38, 40, 53, 60, 64, 74–77, 108, 141
Man of Destiny, The, 11, 67–68
The Matter with Ireland, 12, 59
Millionairess, The, 114–15, 141
"Miraculous Revenge, The," 54
Misalliance, 32, 41, 42, 85–87, 90, 111
Mrs Warren's Profession, 11, 38, 63–64, 67, 101, 140
Music in London, 12
My Dear Dorothea, 44

On the Rocks, 108, 111–12, 131
Our Theatres in the Nineties, 12
Overruled, 90

Passion Play, 9, 60–61
Passion, Poison and Petrifaction, 90
Perfect Wagnerite, The, 44, 58
Philanderer, The, 11, 41, 62–63
Platform and Pulpit, 12, 101, 136
Plays, Pleasant and Unpleasant, 63
The Playwright and the Pirate: Bernard Shaw and Frank Harris, 15
Portable Bernard Shaw, 13, 53
Press Cuttings, 90
Pygmalion, 10, 24, 29, 41, 50, 60, 91–94, 95, 125, 134

Quintessence of Ibsenism, The, 17, 18, 44, 57, 58, 66

Rationalization of Russia by Bernard Shaw, The, 13
Religious Speeches of Bernard Shaw, The, 12, 45, 101
Road to Equality: Ten Unpublished Lectures and Essays, 1884–1918, The, 13

Saint Joan, 10, 25, 35, 38, 39, 54, 91, 102–8, 109, 119, 122, 125, 130, 131, 132, 138
Salt of the Earth, The, 54
Selected Nondramatic Writings of Bernard Shaw, 13
Shakes versus Shav, 116, 120, 125, 138
Sham Education, 12
Shaw: An Autobiography 1856–1898, 20
Shaw: An Autobiography. The Playwright Years 1898–1950, 20
Shaw and Society: An Anthology and a Symposium, 12
Shaw on Dickens, 16
Shaw on Religion, 13, 45
Shaw on Shakespeare, 116
Shaw on Theatre, 12, 112
Shaw's Music, 16, 56
Shewing-Up of Blanco Posnet, The, 9, 84, 88
Short Stories, Scraps and Shavings, 12
Simpleton of the Unexpected Isles, The, 29, 112–13
Six of Calais, The, 111
Sixteen Self Sketches, 12, 20
"Some Necessary Repairs to Religion," 40
"St. James's Hall Mystery, The," 54
Standard Edition (Constable), 12

Table-talk of G.B.S.: Conversations on Things in General between George Bernard Shaw and His Biographer, 12
Three Plays for Puritans, 72, 73
To a Young Actress: The Letters of Bernard Shaw to Molly Tompkins, 15
Too True To Be Good, 25, 99, 109–11
Translations and Tomfooleries, 89–91

Unfinished Novel by Bernard Shaw, An, 31, 51, 53, 124
Unsocial Socialist, An, 52, 53, 57, 75

Village Wooing, 111

What I Really Wrote about the War, 12, 59
Why She Would Not, 120
Widowers' Houses, 11, 33, 61, 85

You Never Can Tell, 11, 21, 69–71

Subject Index

acting and actors, 24, 107
alphabet and alphabet reform, 27, 46
art criticism and artists, 16, 27, 57, 69, 72, 111, 133
authorship, 31, 34–35
autobiography, 19–20, 28, 32, 52, 86–87, 90

Bible, The (*see also* religion), 96, 100–101
biography, 20–24
boxing, 27, 30–31

capitalism (and market economy), 99, 136
censorship and press freedom, 85, 105, 136
charity and philanthropy, 80
children (*see under* parent-child relationships)
communism (*see under* Marxism)
copyright and copyright practice, 6
creative evolution, 44–45, 72, 76, 82, 104, 113

death (and funerals), 100–101, 106
dictators and dictatorship (*see also under* related political movements), 115, 117
drama criticism, 12, 16, 17–18, 58–59, 66, 85–86
dreams and dream-plays, 32, 75, 86–87, 98
drinking, alcoholism, and teetotalism, 80

education, 12, 44, 64, 136

Fabian Society (*see also under* individual members by name), 12, 17, 23, 31–32, 124, 136, 137
family and family relationships, 25, 29, 32, 86–87
fascism, 115, 116–18
feminism (*see under* women and women's rights)
fiction and fiction writing, 51–55, 114
fictional representations of Shaw, 103, 124–27

films and film scripts, 10, 50, 91–92, 105
friends and friendships (*see under* individual names)

heredity and genetics, 82

imprisonment and punishment, 12

leaders and leadership, 71–73, 102–8, 112, 117–18, 118–19
letters and letter writing, 14–16, 32, 125
Life Force (*see under* creative evolution)
literary criticism, 16, 27, 57, 137
love affairs (of Shaw's), 125–26

marriage and marital relationships, 28, 62, 74, 84–85, 115
Marxism, 13, 22, 30, 48, 83–84, 107, 111–12, 114–15, 140–41
medicine and doctors, 82–84, 110
monarchy, 108–9, 118–19
municipal politics and issues, 135–36, 137
music and music criticism, 12, 16, 40, 56, 67, 75
myth and the use of myth, 73, 75–77, 87, 94, 95, 100–101, 134

oratory (*see* speaking, public)

parent-child relationships, 32, 64, 70, 86–87, 89, 90
phonetics (*see also under* alphabet), 93
photography, 13
playwriting and playwrights (*see also under* drama criticism), 9–13, 37–38, 63, 79, 86, 87, 90, 91, 104, 120
poetry and verse, 14, 86

radio, Shaw's involvement with, 136
religion (*see also* particular religions), 12–13, 15, 40–41, 45, 60–61, 69, 73, 78–79, 80–82, 87, 88, 101, 102–8, 110, 113, 136

saints and saintliness, 81–82, 102–8
science-fiction, 100, 126
sex and sexual morals, 26, 27, 28, 29, 30, 64, 109
Shakespeare, attitude toward, 72, 89, 115–16, 137, 138
socialism (*see under* Marxism)
speaking, public, 11–12, 17, 27, 28, 30, 45
style (in writing), 34–35, 40, 45–46, 77

travels (by Shaw), 13, 28, 53

vegetarianism, 27, 126

war, 12, 35, 59, 68, 95, 97, 107, 111, 117–18, 136–37
will and testament, last, 4–5
women and women's rights, 28, 42–43, 74, 76–77, 90, 136